SAR DIN IA

T0001610

Travel with Marco Polo Insider Tips

INSIDER TIP
Your shortcut to a great experience

MARCO POLO TOP HIGHLIGHTS

MONTE LIMBARA ⭐
From a woodland of cork oaks, climb to the roof of Gallura to see as far as Corsica on a clear day.

➤ p. 47, The Northeast

ASINARA ⭐
Serious criminals were once held on Sardinia's version of Alcatraz, but now the island is only home to white donkeys.

➤ p. 71, The Northwest

CAGLIARI ⭐
On the old castle mount, you'll find chic palaces, Sardinian dolce vita and the most beautiful square on the island.
📷 *Tip: You'll get the best perspective of the cathedral by descending the steps to Piazza Carlo Alberto.*

➤ p. 88, The South

PUNTA LA MARMORA ⭐
The ascent of Sardinia's highest mountain is no walk in the park, but the long-distance views from the summit are breathtaking.
📷 *Tip: Stay overnight on the mountain and set your camera to record the time-lapse between sunset and sunrise.*

➤ p. 121, The Interior

VILLASIMIUS ⭐
A beach paradise that's so beautiful, everyone wants to come here – and the great thing is, there's enough room for all! (photo)
📷 *Tip: Climb up to the Saracen tower in Porto Giunco for a great setting, with beach, lagoon and mountains in the background.*

➤ p. 95, The South

COSTA VERDE ⭐
The "Sahara of Sardinia" has Europe's highest dunes and is just the place for those who enjoy solitude.

📷 *Tip: Use the sport or slow-motion setting to capture the experience of rolling or sliding down the dunes.*

➤ p. 84, The South

ALGHERO'S OLD TOWN ⭐
This place is not typical at all: in Alghero, Sardinia meets Catalonia. The influence of the coastal town's former occupiers is still very much in evidence.

➤ p. 67, The Northwest

MURALS IN ORGOSOLO ⭐
Expressive visual depictions of shepherds, oppression and Sardinian self-confidence.

➤ p. 117, The Interior

GROTTA DI ISPINIGOLI ⭐
A dream world of stalactites and cave walls, lit up in many colours.

➤ p. 106, The East Coast

ISOLA DI SAN PIETRO ⭐
Shoals of tuna, a Ligurian population and bizarre coastal cliffs formed from volcanic lava.

📷 *Tip: Capo Sandalo is the perfect spot to take photos of the landscape at sunset.*

➤ p. 87, The South

CONTENTS

CONTENTS

⏱ Plan your visit

€ – €€€ Price categories

(*) Premium-rate phone number

🍴 Eating/drinking

👜 Shopping

🍸 Going out

🏖 Top beaches

☂ Rainy day activities

🐷 Budget activities

👪 Family activities

⚑ Classic experiences

(🗺 A2) Refers to the removable pull-out map
(0) Located off the map

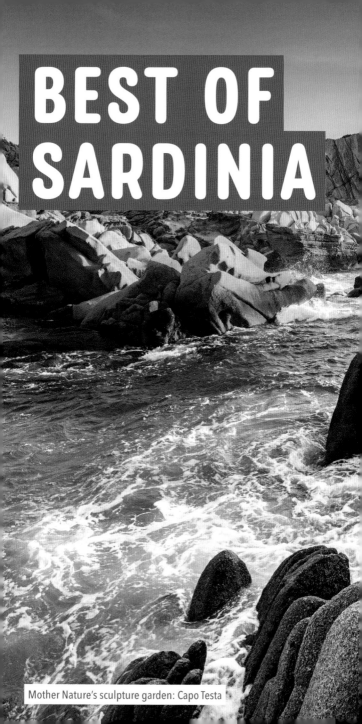

BEST OF
SARDINIA

Mother Nature's sculpture garden: Capo Testa

BEST WHEN IT RAINS

ACTIVITIES TO BRIGHTEN YOUR DAY

FORDONGIANUS THERMAL BATHS

Even the ancient Romans refreshed themselves in these sulphurous thermal springs. The *Bagni Termali Comunali* were built around 1800 and are open to visitors. Pay a small fee and luxuriate in the hot water at 43°C.
➤ p. 80, The South

MUSEUM OF SARDINIAN KNIVES

Located in a historic forge in Arbus, the *Museo del Coltello Sardo* offers visitors the opportunity to watch how a Sardinian knife is produced (photo).
➤ p. 85, The South

CAGLIARI'S CITADEL MUSEUMS

The former citadel now houses no fewer than five museums. Among these is the *National Archaeological Museum*, which promises an exciting trip through the prehistory and early history of the island.
➤ p. 90, The South

A LEISURELY RIDE THROUGH THE COUNTRYSIDE

The island was once criss-crossed by a network of narrow-gauge railway tracks. Today some of the most scenic sections are run as seasonal tourist routes. A ride on the *Trenino Verde*, perhaps from Arbatax to Sadali, is an unforgettable experience.
➤ p. 105, The East Coast

SARDINIAN FOLK CULTURE

Immerse yourself in the rich traditions and folk art of Sardinia at the *Museo Etnografico Sardo* in Nuoro. In addition to a fabulous collection of costumes – every village has its own – there is an exhibition about the art of Sardinian breadmaking, with more than 600 different examples. Unfortunately, they're only for show.
➤ p. 115, The Interior

BEST 🐷 ON A BUDGET

FOR SMALLER WALLETS

ENJOY COSTA SMERALDA STYLE FOR FREE

A high point of neo-Sardinian Costa Smeralda architecture is the church of *Stella Maris* (photo) in Porto Cervo. Head inside to admire the genuine El Greco painting. The top-quality view of the marina is also free.

➤ p. 48, The Northeast

NATURE'S SCULPTURE GARDEN

Completely free of charge and easily accessible, the *Capo Testa* (photo p.6) at Santa Teresa di Gallura is a fairy-tale world of whimsical rock formations that you can explore to your heart's content. Don't forget to take a towel for the idyllic beach coves.

➤ p. 55, The Northeast

CAVING FOR FREE

The *Grotta di San Giovanni* at Domusnovas is a unique natural tunnel that has been hollowed out of the mountain over time by a stream. A road was laid through the tunnel, but it's now only open to walkers and cyclists.

➤ p. 85, The South

MOUNTAIN TERRAIN IN A NATURE RESERVE

Marked trails lead through the wild, romantic and mountainous landscape of the *Parco dei Sette Fratelli*, punctuated by picnic spots. An information centre at the entrance provides route maps, and the free *Museo Cervo Sardo* has information about the rare endemic Sardinian deer.

➤ p. 97, The South

SPOT WILD HORSES

There really are wild horses on Sardinia! They roam the isolated cork oak woods of the *Giara di Gesturi* plateau and the *Foresta Demaniale di Porto Conte* nature park.

➤ p. 122, The Interior, and p. 70, The Northwest

BEST

WITH CHILDREN

SNORKELLING FOR ALL

Orso Diving will take children who can swim to the dive site on *Archipelago di La Maddalena* for a snorkelling session. Young divers are given a thorough safety briefing and are equipped with a mask, snorkel and fins. The inflatable boat trip out to the diving spot is all part of the adventure.
➤ p. 33, Sport & activities

FLUMES, SLIDES & RAINBOW COLOURS

Sardinia's best-known waterpark is *Aquadream* on the Costa Smeralda. Every Saturday it hosts a fun session with coloured body paints. It's a good job that there's a foam party right next door, so that you can wash off the mess afterwards.
➤ p. 49, The Northeast

PERFECT POOLS

Who says that you need a beach or a hotel pool in order to go swimming?

The *Piscine Naturali von Coccorrocci* consist of natural pools with mini waterfalls, making them perfect for family bathing.
➤ p. 105, The East Coast

RURAL HISTORY & FURRY FRIENDS

Discover the hardships and deprivations of Sardinian rural life in times gone by at the *S'Abba Frisca* show farm near Dorgali. Afterwards, the little ones can stroke the donkeys, while the grown-ups sample the own-brand olive oil.
➤ p. 106, The East Coast

SARDINIA IN MINIATURE

First, hop in a boat for a trip past Sardinia's most famous sights; then, it's off to the planetarium and the dinosaur park. All this is possible at *Sardegna in Miniatura,* a paradise for children.
➤ p. 122, The Interior

BEST ⚑

CLASSIC EXPERIENCES

PECORINO & PANE CARASAU

Paper-thin flatbread (photo) and aromatic sheep's cheese are the staple fare for local shepherds. They're both still made by hand, following time-honoured traditions, especially in inland Sardinia, and they're served as *antipasti* all over Sardinia.

➤ p. 26, Eating & drinking

VERMENTINO & CANNONAU

Sardinian winemakers have taken an enormous leap forward in terms of quality, producing excellent red and white wines, some of which have achieved international cult status. Typically, Sardinian varieties include the straw-yellow Vermentino and the dark red Cannonau.

➤ p. 28, Eating & drinking

SHEPHERD'S KNIFE

Every boy longs to have one, and every Sardinian man proudly carries one – a Sardinian shepherd's pocketknife. In the past, nearly every village had its own cutler; today only a few villages continue the knife-maker's art, such as *Arbus* and *Pattada*.

➤ p. 30, Shopping

BOAT TRIP IN A NATIONAL PARK

When you're on an island, what could be more appealing than a boat trip? The most beautiful destination is *La Maddalena national park*, an archipelago between Sardinia and Corsica.

➤ p. 52, The Northeast

FAIRY HOUSES

All over Sardinia you'll spot cave openings, known as *domus de janas*, or "fairy houses". These are prehistoric burial tombs hewn into the rock. One of the most impressive is *Montessu necropolis*, which stretches across two hills. You can walk for hours through this peaceful landscape between the numerous grottoes and graves.

➤ p. 86, The South

GET TO KNOW SARDINIA

Traditional costumes are still worn for festivals: Sartiglia in Oristano

DISCOVER SARDINIA

Discover coves and donkeys on Asinara in the northwest

People tend to go misty-eyed as soon as they hear about Sardinia. First, there are the beaches. Once you've paddled in the sea at Cala Brandinchi near San Teodoro, you no longer need the Caribbean; once you've explored the dreamy bays on the Golfo di Orosei, you just know you will return there.

REST & RELAXATION

Of course, thanks to its Mediterranean climate and 1,900km of coast, which has countless picture-perfect beaches and coves, Sardinia is above all a wonderful destination for a beach holiday. But there's much more to it than that: the unspoilt nature of Sardinia's wild mountains make them a paradise for hikers and mountain bikers. They're also the ideal place to unwind in solitude and

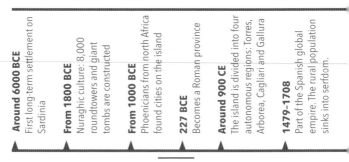

Around 6000 BCE
First long-term settlement on Sardinia

From 1800 BCE
Nuraghic culture: 8,000 roundtowers and giant tombs are constructed

From 1000 BCE
Phoenicians from north Africa found cities on the island

227 BCE
Becomes a Roman province

Around 900 CE
The island is divided into four autonomous regions: Torres, Arborea, Cagliari and Gallura

1479–1708
Part of the Spanish global empire. The rural population sinks into serfdom.

silence; the peace is broken only by the tinkling of bells from flocks of sheep and goats that roam the countryside day in and day out.

The sheer variety of landscapes on this island is what makes Sardinia so enticing: rugged granite outcrops in Gallura; eroded limestone rocks in the Supramonte; windswept gorse bushes on the stormy west coast; thickly forested mountain slopes in the Gennargentu…. And when the sunset intensifies the colours of the red coastal cliffs on the Costa Paradiso, then you'll know you're somewhere extraordinary.

How about a sundowner on Alghero's city walls? You'll see the sun setting behind the limestone cliffs of the Capo Caccia, creating a silhouette that resembles a sleeping old man with a pot belly. But this doesn't mark the end of your Sardinian day – evenings are the best time to get to know the island's inhabitants.

MEETING THE LOCALS

Your encounters with local Sardinians will be a defining feature of your holiday – whether that's a family on the beach at the weekend, a shepherd in the mountains, or the winemaker, the chef and the bartender that serve you food and drink. Their proud reserve and unrivalled hospitality are as much a reflection of the island's character as its ancient songs, strange melodies and seemingly melancholic traditional circle dances.

The pride and dedication that the Sardinians devote to maintaining their

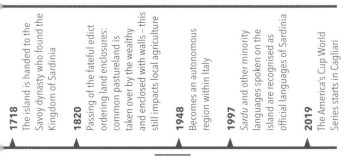

1718
The island is handed to the Savoy dynasty who found the Kingdom of Sardinia

1820
Passing of the fateful edict ordering land enclosures: common pastureland is taken over by the wealthy and enclosed with walls – this still impacts local agriculture

1948
Becomes an autonomous region within Italy

1997
Sardu and other minority languages spoken on the island are recognised as official languages of Sardinia

2019
The America's Cup World Series starts in Cagliari

traditions is matched by the attention and love they give to their cuisine, which, by the way, you'll get to know better in the interior than on the coast. Here it is not uncommon for visitors to be spontaneously invited to one of the numerous village festivals and to be welcomed warmly into the community. And there is no lack of opportunity, since over 1,000 festivals take place across the island each year, celebrating everything from the harvest and sheep-shearing to saints or horse riding. Once the Sardinians get started on the heavy red wine and start singing about the old ways, you'll soon work up an appetite. Fortunately, Sardinia has much more to offer than pizza and spaghetti.

TO FIND THE REAL SARDINIA, HEAD INLAND

Sardinia has been conquered over and over again. The Phoenicians were the first invaders to land on the island in the ninth century CE. In the centuries that followed, the islanders were subjected to a succession of foreign rulers, who had nothing else in mind but to enslave the local population and to exploit the island's riches and mineral resources. In response, the Sardinians retreated from the coasts into the wild and inaccessible mountains, turning their back on the sea and the world. And so Sardinia became an island of farmers and shepherds, whose villages remained so isolated from each other even into the 20th century that countless regional dialects developed. Until the late 20th century, the island was also a much-feared place of exile; the remote penal island of Asinara, known as the Italian Alcatraz, wasn't closed until 1998.

FROM LUXURY DESTINATION TO HOLIDAY PARADISE FOR ALL

When the Aga Khan, one of the world's richest people, opened up the beautiful northeast tip of the island to the international jet set at the beginning of the 1960s, he broke into an archaic world which was still governed by the traditional principles of honour, family and community. And so, for a long time, the luxury resorts remained a world apart; they had little to do with Sardinia or the Sardinians and were only animated for a short six-week holiday season. The name Costa Smeralda was conceived in the marketing departments of international investment houses and, like a capital investment, the celebrity exclusivity was also protected. Yet, thanks to light-touch coastal architecture that resembles natural forms, Sardinia has been spared the worst excesses of the concrete building boom that marred other Mediterranean resorts: sprawling coastal developments are a rarity here.

With the advent of cheap flights, Sardina became ever more popular as a holiday destination. Of course, there are examples of tourist excess even here: increasing numbers of Airbnb apartments in Alghero and Cagliari are displacing old-town residents, just as they are in Berlin and Barcelona. Nevertheless, the island's deeply traditional population still regards hospitality as one of the highest virtues and considers it an honour to treat guests with honesty and respect.

AT A GLANCE

1,648,000
population

Lancashire: 1,515,000

270 km
Average distance north to south

145 km
Average distance east to west

1,230 km
Length of coastline (excluding offshore islands)

Length of Irish coastline: 3,171 km

24,089 km²
area

Wales: 20,779 km²

Highest mountain:
Punta La Marmora

1,834 m

ONLY NAVIGABLE RIVER

Temo

55 km in length

But only 6km near Bosa are navigable

APPROXIMATE NUMBER OF NURAGHI

7,000

FAMOUS VISITORS

Princess Diana; George Clooney (once dated the Sardinian model Elisabetta Canalis); Sir Elton John; Lindsay Lohan; Sean Penn

£425 million

Most expensive holiday home: Villa Certosa owned by Silvio Berlusconi in Porto Rotondo

OLDEST SARDINIAN
ANTONIO TODDE, WHO DIED IN 2002 AGED 112

Between 1996 and 2016, the Sardinian village of Seulo had 20 residents aged over 100

UNDERSTAND SARDINIA

INDEPENDENT SARDINIA?

Graffiti along the highway proclaims: *Sa Sardigna no est s'Italia: indipendèntzia!* – "Sardinia is not Italy: independence!" Many Sardinians are of the view that their island should be an independent state. But what such a state would look like is hotly contested, with about as many differing opinions as there are villages on the island. Roughly speaking, they want educational and cultural autonomy, control of their own finances and the right to use their own language. Frustration at Rome's condescension is particularly strong around issues on which Sardinia has had no say in the past: the establishment of heavy industry on the island, for example, or the creation of huge military exclusion areas which have turned Sardinia into an "unsinkable aircraft carrier". This frustration, combined with a lack of clear policies, has helped Italian protest parties to gain increasing support on the island. Luckily, the situation is not as volatile as on the neighbouring island of Corsica. So far, the protests have remained non-violent; here, it's still *murales* that do the talking instead of bombs.

SHEPHERD: JOB OR VOCATON?

They don't need to go to the gym because hand-milking is still the done thing here and, as their muscular forearms prove, that's a better workout than any dumb-bell. If you see a man in dusty jeans downing a cappuccino or a Sardinian Ichnusa beer at five in the morning, remember that he quite probably owns hectares of land. The Sardinian shepherd must tend his flock and produce cheese and ricotta, a good proportion of which is made out in the wilderness rather than in a dairy, even today.

It all sounds wildly romantic, but bear in mind that for Sardinia's 30,000 shepherds it is more than just a job – this is a calling whose skills are passed from generation to generation. Thanks to cars and roads, young shepherds are no longer denied a social life, and they live in modern apartment blocks instead of the traditional *pineddas* – simple stone huts built to protect shepherds from the elements, with a pitched roof made from branches and an open fire pit. As the old shepherds pass on, so the picturesque figures in their velvet suits, with tight-fitting peaked caps on their heads, become a thing of the past. The new generation prefers jeans or outfits from the military surplus stores.

With more than five million sheep, Sardinia has by far the greatest number of any Italian region. The island produces around 80% of the country's hugely popular high-quality pecorino sheep's cheese. If you're in the middle of nowhere and you see the sign, "Vendita Formaggi", be sure to stop the car. And it's also worth trying the produce that is sold directly from the boot of an old Fiat Panda, say, in a beach car park – it's likely to be the real deal, as the strong smell with testify. But watch out: pecorino should be stored at temperatures under 15°C, so don't keep it in your beach bag!

WHITE ELEPHANTS

There's no better way to describe the many failed industrialisation projects that took place on Sardinia in the second half of the 20th century. The large petroleum refineries in Porto Torres and the Gulf of Cagliari, the chemical fibre plant at Ottana, the aluminium smelters at Portoscuso and the paper factory at Arbatax were all used to lure voters in elections, but they have delivered very few secure or high-quality jobs. What's more, they produce little for the Sardinian market; they harm the island's environment, and they are constantly threatened with closure. A large proportion now stand empty and abandoned and are blots on the landscape.

CLOTHES FROM CORK

The cork oak is the island's most characteristic tree. It resembles a holm oak, but the leaves and the acorns are somewhat smaller, while the bark, in contrast, is sturdy and knobbly. When the tree reaches a certain age, a horizontal split appears in the bark of the upper tree, revealing the dark red trunk underneath – it looks rather as though the tree is taking its trousers off. Cork is still gathered by hand, in high summer when the bark is dry. A cork tree is first stripped of its bark when it reaches the age of 45, or thereabouts; from then on, the stripping takes place once every nine to 12 years. Sardinian cork is not only used for wine corks and crafts, but also for

Every nine to 12 years, the cork oaks in the Gallura are ready for stripping

Virtual reality from the analogue era: *mural* in San Sperate

floor tiles, insulation panels, furniture, mousepads, book covers and, believe it or not, designer clothing and bags that have made it onto international catwalks. The patent for the "vegetable fibres" is owned by Anna Grindi from Tempio Pausania, who spent years being ridiculed for her attempts but has now realised her dream of creating a cork-based fabric. Sardinia is the third-biggest producer of cork in Europe, after Portugal and Spain. Around 10 per cent of all the cork in the world comes from the small community of Calangianus in Gallura, which has around 200 cork manufacturers.

CONSERVATION

Gone with the wind: discarded flyers flutter through the streets and plastic bottles roll into the gutters. Separating rubbish for recycling has been obligatory across the island for a few years now, but Sardinians are yet to fully embrace the sustainability message. The authorities have made the effort to ban plastic bags in supermarkets – instead there are alternatives made from corn starch which you must pay for. The island's annual forest fires are often caused by carelessness, and some are even set deliberately.

SARDINIAN STREET ART

The murals that decorate the walls of houses in Orgosolo and Villagrande Strisaili are striking and usually easy to understand; they combine depictions of Sardinia's past and present, with the hope of a better and unconditionally Sardinian future. The initial impetus came from the Italian student protest movement after 1968:

politically engaged young artists got to know the murals of Mexico and Chile, and also adopted the Spanish word *murales*. Later, local amateurs also took up their brushes and paints. At first, the themes came from the Sardinian independence movement, protesting against the sell-out of the island to the military and tourism companies. But there were also subjects from Sardinian history, depicting the world of the eternal underdog and the bitter conflicts between landowners and rural workers. The *murales* in villages such as San Sperate, Serramanna and Tinnura feature high-quality trompe l'oeil effects, with the walls depicting realistic village scenes that entice the viewer into a virtual visual world.

ANDIAMO AL MARE

Sardinia's beaches are the number one destination for most visitors, and for good reason; their beauty and abundance means that comparisons with a Caribbean island are no exaggeration. Apart from a few areas around the large ports and industrial zones, the sea is clear and clean and most beaches remain pristine and unspoiled. The northern and western coasts are exposed to the strong winds of the mistral, making them perfect for wind- and kitesurfers; the eastern and southern coastlines are much calmer. For northern Europeans, used to the North Sea or the Atlantic, sea swimming is pleasant from May onwards, but most Italians prefer to wait until July before taking a dip. The water remains a reasonable temperature

TRUE OR FALSE?

SARDINIA IS EXPENSIVE
Granted, if you want to bomb around the island in a luxury car, stay in a mega-villa and cruise around on a super-yacht, then you can spend a fortune on the Costa Smeralda. But make the most of early-booking discounts, hire a Fiat instead of a Ferrari, avoid high season and hotels with private beaches, and you won't spend noticeably more on Sardinia than on any other Mediterranean island.

SARDINIA IS FULL OF BANDITS
Malicious rumours suggest that some solo travellers have journeyed to Orgosolo only to be kidnapped by bandits. In fact, this notion of outlaws roaming Sardinia is limited to a few isolated incidents in the Barbagia mountains, where vans transporting money have been held up after finding their way blocked with logs. The concept of the vendetta is also often wrongly characterised as some kind of blood revenge. In fact, the rules that govern society in the Barbagia are not about arbitrary conflicts between families, but rather unwritten laws that control how people interact with each other in an area of the country that the local *carabinieri* (police) avoid to this day. Even when these laws concern a serious matter, blood rarely flows.

into October or November, although the south is always a few degrees warmer than the north of the island at this time.

What's more, all the beaches on Sardinia are freely accessible to everyone. As long as you're not put off by the prospect of a body search, in theory you can lie down on the sand in front of a villa belonging to the super-rich. And don't be annoyed if your dream beach is occasionally covered in metres of sea-grass (*posidonia*); it can't be cleared for environmental reasons because it contributes to the health of the Mediterranean for fish and sea creatures. With a bit of luck and the right wind, the situation will look completely different a few days later. Many beaches are not signposted and are difficult to find. One way of identifying your personal favourite is to consult the helpful beach guide on *sardinianbeaches.com*, which maps out all the beaches on the island that are suitable for swimming.

SA LIMBA SARDA

The Sardinian language is not an Italian dialect but a recognised independent tongue and, since 1997, the island's second offical language. The problem is that there are almost as many different dialects of spoken Sardinian as there are hills and villages on the island. And while Sardinian poems and sayings are as plentiful as the rocks in Gallura, Sardinian songs are sung at rural festivals. Many communities have two village signposts: the one in Sardinian is new and fresh; the one in Italian, by contrast, is often shot through with holes. But don't worry, daily life proceeds peacefully: if a Sardinian meets someone who doesn't speak the language, they'll automatically switch to formal Italian.

WATER OF LIFE

Month-long droughts are not uncommon in the summer and bring with them a heightened risk of forest and scrub fires. The situation becomes particularly severe in those years when the customary winter rains stay away and the weather remains much too mild and dry. When this happens, the springs dry up and crops wither in the pastures and fields. Tourists are unlikely to feel the impact of this water shortage in the holiday resorts, but visitors should be respectful of the situation and not spend ages under the shower, for example. Mountain and forest springs are often besieged by locals with jerrycans and large flasks, because the fresh water tastes better than the tap water, which is often treated with chlorine. Try it for yourself.

QUATTRO MORI

You'll see the Sardinian flag, with its *quattro mori* – the so-called "Four Moors", fluttering in the wind everywhere, from the town hall to the beach kiosk. And the figures on the flag generate a lot of discussion: sometimes they're wearing headbands, sometimes, blindfolds; they may be looking to the left or to the right. What is little known today is that the flag is the symbol of sovereignty of the Aragonese, who ruled the island from the 14th century and brought their banner with them. And, although that far-distant era wasn't a particularly positive time for the Sardinians, in the intervening centuries the *quattro mori* has become as much a symbol of the island as the Ichnusa beer, which sports the *quattro mori* as its logo.

ISLAND OF TOWERS

Around a hundred towers are spread around the Sardinian coast. The so-called "Saracen Towers" were built between the 15th and 18th centuries in order to repel attacks by pirates (Saracens), who plundered villages, even those far inland, abducting their inhabitants and selling them into slavery. Even more spectacular are, without doubt, the *nuraghi*: mighty Megalithic cone-shaped towers that take their name from the nuraghic civilisation that created them. This fascinating Bronze Age culture is characterised by its prolific building and sculpture work. More than 7,000 complete or partially extant *nuraghi* stand on the island; many have only the foundation walls remaining while others have three storeys that reach heights of over 12m. Some are used as shelters or folds for sheep. They are positioned within sight of one another along mountain ridges or on the edge of plateaux to form defensive lines, as is clearly visible at Macomer and around the Giara di Gesturi. In addition, there are hundreds of grave sites (so-called "giant tombs"), diverse small temples dedicated to the water cult (holy springs) and thousands of bronze figures representing warriors, pilgrims, priests, animals, boats and nuraghi.

How on earth did they build that?! You'll be astounded by the island's nuraghi

EATING
SHOPPING
SPORT

Loved by gourmets but not by swimmers: sea urchins

EATING & DRINKING

Even though pizza and spaghetti feature on the menu, true Sardinian cuisine is very different from that on the Italian mainland. Shepherds, farmers and fishermen all have their own culinary traditions.

Bread beats pasta as Sardinia's main staple. In the rural villages of the interior, where many families still do their own baking, you'll find versions of a thin crispy flatbread: in its paper-thin round form it is called ⚑ *pane carasau* (the Italians call this *carta di musica* – music paper); the slightly chunkier rectangular version is known as *pane pistoccu*. To make *pane frattau*, or "Sardinian pizza", the *pane pistoccu* is soaked in broth and topped with tomato sauce, cheese and a poached egg. Watch out for supermarket-bought bread, which tends to be low quality; instead buy freshly baked goods from a *panetteria* or a *forno*.

PASTA & PIZZA

Pasta is an integral part of Sardinian cuisine. Although spaghetti originates from mainland Italy, it is very popular here and has even begun to displace more traditional Sardinian pastas in day-to-day cooking. Traditional pastas include *malloreddus*, a type of gnocchi that is usually served with a fennel sausage ragù, or the tiny hand-rolled semolina dough balls known as *fregola*.

If you fancy a pizza, your best bet is to head for a venue that's busy with locals as this means it's earned its stripes as a pizzeria. Venues that announce "*pizza a pranzo*" ("lunchtime pizza") are likely to be **INSIDER TIP Pizza pitfall** tourist traps. The latest trend is for "Pizza Gourmet" outlets, which sell pizza slices laden with high-quality ingredients – they're ideal for a quick lunch or a snack, but they're not cheap.

Cannonau is the leading Sardinian red grape variety (right)

BARBECUE FEASTS

Large-scale open-air banquets are often held on Sundays and special occasions. Hours before it's time to eat, the meat is set to spit-roast over hot coals and the aroma of suckling pig and lamb begins to waft through the forest. Juniper, myrtle and rosemary twigs in the embers lend the smoke its herbal fragrance, but the real seasoning comes from the herbs that the animals have grazed on in the pastures. This traditional Sardinian barbecue is a resolutely male affair. Old men watch over the roast, ensuring that the crackling is crispy and golden-brown and the meat is juicy and aromatic. Strong Cannonau red wine keeps their energy levels high during the long hours of preparation and roasting.

A carraxiau, the legendary pit roast, is the most famous of all Sardinian specialities. First, a huge fire is burnt in a pit in the ground, and then the meat is slow roasted on the embers. This unusual method probably has its roots in the widespread theft of livestock. When rustlers wanted to feast on a snatched lamb, they would light a seemingly innocent fire to camouflage the embers in the hole in the ground below.

SAY CHEESE

The aroma of the sparse but herb-rich pastures also goes into Sardinian cheese, which is usually made from sheep's milk and ranges in texture from creamy and soft to rock hard. The classic ⌐ *pecorino sardo* is a sheep's cheese, which can either be *fresco*, meaning it is just one or two months old and has a mild taste, or *stagionato*, which means it has matured for at least six months to gain a strong, punchy flavour.

An old tradition is the production of pungent *casu marzu,* in which fly larvae transform the hard cheese into a spreadable cream; the larvae are then eaten live along with the cheese. This is certainly not everybody's cup of tea. You won't find *casu marzu* available for sale because production is banned. Less adventurous palates will enjoy the variety of mild cheeses on offer, such as *dolce sardo*, a soft cheese made from cow's milk; fresh and mild ricotta, best made from sheep's milk, or *ricotta salata* with its salty, acidic taste. The last of these goes particularly well with honey; for example, the famous bitter *miele amaro* made from the nectar of the *corbezzolo* or strawberry tree *(Arbutus unedo)*.

FRESH FISH

Fish is at its finest when fresh off the boat, roasted on the charcoal grill and sparingly seasoned with aromatic herbs and a little garlic. This method is used for everything from the meaty mullet *(muggine, cefalo)* to cheap sardines *(sarde);* you'll smell the delicious aroma coming from fishermen's picnics on the beach.

FROM PLONK TO PRIZE-WINNING WINES

For decades, Sardinian wine was virtually unknown, as most of the production was for the mass market bottling of "wines from various EU countries". This has changed enormously in recent years, ever since an increasing number of winemakers began working with leading oenologists to bring high-quality wines to the market. Many are now highly prized in international wine circles.

Without doubt, the top Sardinian wine is the red Turriga produced by Cantina Argiolas in Serdiana; close behind it is the Korem, another red. The Terre Brune and Rocca Rubia reds from the Cantina di Santadi also have an international reputation. The ⚑ Cannonau is the classic Sardinian red wine grape, and the best version is the heavy Nepente produced by the Cantina di Oliena.

The best white wines are cultivated in the Gallura region around Monti, Berchidda and Arzachena; the ⚑ Vermentino is the most famous variety. The undisputed number one among Sardinian whites is, however, the Capichera, a wine that is as fine as it is expensive; it's a fixture on the wine lists of high-dining restaurants on the Costa Smeralda. Some superb dessert wines are grown in the west of Sardinia, most notably the Malvasia from Bosa, Sorso and Sennori, and the Vernaccia di Oristano, from the Tirso valley.

FINISH WITH A *DIGESTIVO*

Sardinian mirto is made from bitter myrtle berries and tends to divide opinion: some people think it tastes like cough mixture; others buy bottles of the strong liquer to take home. There's no mistaking the strength of Filu 'e Ferru, since the name of this Sardinian grappa is literally "iron wire". The name comes from the time when illicit alcohol was buried to keep it hidden; in order to find it again, a thin iron wire was tied to the bottle.

Today's Recommendations

Antipasti

PANE GUTTIAU
Sardinian flatbread with salt and olive oil

INSALATA DI POLPO
Octopus salad with potato, celery, garlic and parsley

ACCIUGHE RIPIENE
Fresh anchovies stuffed with soft cheese, coated in breadcrumbs and oven-baked

Primi Piatti

FREGOLA CON ARSELLE E BOTTARGA
Beads of semolina pasta served with clams and dried mullet roe

RAVIOLI DI BIETOLA E RICOTTA
Ravioli filled with Swiss chard and ricotta

MACCARRONES FURRIAOS
Pasta with cheese curd

CULURGIONES
Stuffed pasta with a potato and mint filling, served with tomato sauce

ZUPPA GALLURESE
Layers of broth-soaked bread and cheese, oven-baked

Secondi

PORCEDDU
Spit-roasted suckling pig with crispy crackling

AGNELLO CON I CARCIOFI
Braised lamb with artichokes

AGNELLO AL FINOCCHIETTO SELVATICO
Lamb stew with fresh wild fennel

CINGHIALE AL FORNO
Oven-roasted wild boar

CORDULA CON PISELLI
Sheep or goat's intestine, stuffed with offal and served with peas

ARAGOSTA ALLA CATALANA
Alghero lobster served with fresh tomatoes and onions

Dolci

PARDULAS
Small baked pastries filled with ricotta and saffron

SEBADAS CON MIELE AMARO
Fried pastry pockets filled with cream cheese and served with bitter honey

PAPASSINOS
Short-crust pastries with raisins and almonds

SHOPPING

AUTHENTIC CRAFTS

In many Sardinian villages, especially in the rural hinterland, you'll still find houses with handlooms at which women weave wool from their flocks into carpets and blankets, following ancient patterns – you may be able to buy the skilful handiwork direct from the makers. In Castelsardo, women sit on the steps in front of the old houses weaving colourful baskets which they sell to the tourists. Bowls, jugs, plates and other ceramics are produced in many places; some follow traditional patterns, others are more modern.

If you want to be sure that you're buying authentic crafts, look out for outlets of the Sardinian Institute for the Promotion of Crafts (I.S.O.L.A.), which only sell certified work by Sardinian artisans. And don't expect to find naff souvenir ornaments that your great-aunt might collect; the modern pottery produced on Sardinia finds its way into the island's most exclusive hotels and boutiques.

WHAT A CORKER!

Loads of souvenirs made from cork can be found all over the island. From postcards to fruit bowls, it seems cork can be added to anything and everything. If there's a bottle of mirto liqueur beneath the cork sleeve, then you can even drink from your cork souvenir.

NOT JUST FOR SHEPHERDS

If the Sardinians themselves could choose a souvenir from their island, it would probably be a ⚑ traditional shepherd's knife from Pattada, Santu Lussurgiu or Arbus, hand-forged from the best steel, with a highly polished handle made from carefully selected horn. It is both a tool and a treasured possession that every Sardinian man carries. Just don't put it in your hand luggage for your journey home.

Castelsardo is a centre for basket-weaving on the island (left)

ALL THINGS BRIGHT & BEAUTIFUL

Exfoliating ointment from ground obsidian, anti-wrinkle cream with coral extract or anti-aging serum with Cannonau grape extracts: these are just some of the products available from *Soha Sardinia*. The business is dedicated to producing high-quality (and correspondingly high-priced) premium cosmetics with Sardinian ingredients – available in all good perfumeries around the island.

SARDINIAN SUPERFOODS

Honey from eucalyptus, orange and strawberry trees is healthy and helps keep colds at bay. When it's added to sweets and biscuits it may also help those suffering from acute Sardinia withdrawal. It's no secret that olive oil is good for you. And some Sardinian centegenarians swear by the life-giving properties of Sardinian red wine. You can buy wine, along with other liquids, at the airport after check-in. An alternative is to do your big shop at *Bonu (Largo Carlo Felice 33 | bonu.it)* in Cagliari the day before your flight,

INSIDER TIP
Carry-on allowance

and then pick up your goodies from their airport shop the next day – they'll count as airport purchases, so you can take them on board as hand luggage.

A BIT OF BLING

You can find silver and gold filigree jewellery in Alghero, Bosa, Gavoi, Nuoro, Dorgali, Iglesias and Cagliari. Avoid buying coral jewellery; coral used to be fished out of the sea off Alghero and Bosa, but these stocks have long been under conservation orders, meaning that the raw material today comes from Southeast Asia.

SPORT & ACTIVITIES

Sardinia and its islands boast over 1,900km of coastline. Water sports, such as snorkelling and diving, sailing and windsurfing, can be enjoyed all around the island. Hiking in the hills or along the coast is a popular pastime in spring and autumn.

In terms of outdoor sports, Sardinia offers a cornucopia of options. Come with a sense of adventure, and you'll find there's plenty to discover beyond the two outdoor centres that currently operate on the island at Dorgali/Cala Gonone and Oliena. Only fit and experienced hikers with good navigation skills should attempt to go it alone, as trails and watering points are not usually signposted, and the sun can be merciless from May to September. If you've got serious trekking ambitions, you're better off entrusting yourself to one of the cooperatives and their local, professionally trained guides.

Detailed information on activities and sporting events can be found at *sardegnaturismo.it*. A number of outdoor activities and excursions are offered by *Sardinia4all (sardinia4all. co.uk/sardinia/excursions)*.

CYCLING

Cycling from the coast up into the mountains is demanding, with climbs of well over 1000m. Bicycles can be transported on most trains and on many of the island's buses. The best contact for both mountain- and road-bike tours in the south is *Dolce Vita Biketours (tel. 07 09 20 98 85 | dolcevitabiketours.com)*. *Oroseinbike (tel. 37 01 32 50 02 | oroseinbike.it)* offers guided mountain bike tours in the Orosei area. In Alghero, Wanny and his team at *Biking Sardinia (tel. 39 33 31 37 88 | bikingsardinia.it)* rent out both pedal bikes and electric bikes and offer guided cycling tours of

Surfing at Capo Mannu on the Sinis Peninsula

Capo Caccia and Asinara. Thanks to the *Ciclovia della Sardegna* project, over 1,000km of cycling routes are being developed across the island. Further information and maps can be found online at *sardegnaciclabile.it*. A comprehensive touring atlas with 24 detailed routes in English can be downloaded from *short.travel/sar6*.

DIVING

Divers and snorkellers find ideal conditions around the island's rocky coasts, particularly at the base of cliffs, where the rocks make the ideal habitat for sea life, with hiding places, nurseries and a good choice of food. 🐾 *Orso Diving (tel. 34 80 64 18 25 | orsodiving.com)* in Poltu Quatu offers diving courses for all abilities at the most beautiful spots around La Maddalena archipelago national park. For wreck and nature dives in the Capo Carbonara marine park, near Villasimius in the southeast of the island, contact the dive school, *Ocean Blue (Kala e Moru | tel. 32 00 51 76 72 | oceanblue-diving. com)*. *Overing Diving Center (tel. 32 75 90 93 00 | archimete.it)* offers snorkelling trips and diving courses at Capo Caccia near Alghero (and a pleasant beach bar for a drink afterwards).

GOLF

Golf is still regarded as an exclusive sport for seniors on Sardinia, although the island's 13 courses are gradually becoming more modern and are beginning to attract a more diverse clientele. The four 18-hole courses are open year-round: *Pevero Golf Club (tel. 07 89 95 80 46 | peverogolfclub. com)* on the Costa Smeralda is the most refined place to swing a club; *Is Molas (tel. 07 09 24 10 06 | ismolas. it)* on the south coast near Santa Margherita di Pula is where international tournaments take place; *Is Arenas Golf Resort (tel. 33 51 25 83 22 | isarenas.it)* on the west coast near Oristano is situated in the middle of a pine forest; while *Tanka Golf (tel. 34 71 72 43 73 | tankagolfvillasimius.it)* affords panoramic views of Villasimius.

HIKING & TREKKING

Sardinia's mountains, its remote high plateaux and the impressive gorges of the Supramonte in the east, around Dorgali, Baunei, Urzulei and Oliena, all provide perfect terrain for hiking. Responsible walkers are advised to join a guided tour with one of the trekking cooperatives operating island-wide. Recommendations include *Keya Tours (tel. 34 86 53 06 82 | keya.eu)* in Orosei and the *Società Gorropu (tel. 33 38 50 71 57 | gorropu.com)* in Urzulei, run by Sandra and Francesco, which provides an information point on the top of the Genna Silana pass. *Your Sardinia (tel. 34 00 06 91 91 | yoursardiniaexperience.it)* organises guided walking tours throughout Sardinia, some of which include overnight stays.

HORSE RIDING

The Sardinians love horses and tend to be excellent riders. There are numerous opportunities to explore the island's countryside on horseback on one- or multi-day excursions. Many *agriturismi* offer riding sessions to their guests. For the best riding on the Costa del Sud, contact *Maneggio di Giancarlo Cabras (tel. 34 87 04 44 47 | cavalcareachia.it)*. In the northeast,

the *Centro Equestre Li Tauli (tel. 39 37 11 59 10 | sardiniahorses.com)* in Cugnana offers excursions along the coast. To the north of the Costa Rei is the *Centro Ippico Sarrabus (tel. 0 70 99 90 78)*. Inland, the *Country Hotel Mandra Edera (tel. 32 01 51 51 70 | facebook.com/mandraedera.cc)* has a riding stables as well as a restaurant and pool.

KAYAKING

When the seas are calm, the steep coast in the east between Orosei, Cala Gonone and Santa Maria Navarrese is ideal for trips by kayak as, unlike the tourist boats, they are small enough to enter the narrowest inlets, smallest coves and hidden sea caves. Guided kayak tours around Alghero are arranged by *Sea Kayak Sardinia (tel. 36 64 97 96 71 | seakayaksardinia.com)*. For relaxing river trips by canoe and kayak along the Riu Coghinas near Valledoria, not far from Castelsardo, contact *New Kayak Sardinia (tel. 33 81 25 84 03 | newkayaksardinia.com)*.

ROCK CLIMBING

The island's most spectacuar climb is the *Via Ferrata del Cabriol* high up on the cliffs of the Capo Caccia near Alghero. Secured with iron ladders, pins or clamps and ropes, the *Ferrata di Giorrè* leads along an almost vertical rock face at Cargeghe, southeast of Sassari. Only highly experienced climbers should attempt the vertical rock face in the *Lanaitho Canyon,* near Oliena. For climbing excursions, contact Sardinia's reliable *via ferrata* specialists, *Corrado Conca (corradoconca.it).*

SAILING

The entire Gallurese coast is ideal for sailing. The Costa Smeralda, the islands of La Maddalena national park and Capo Testa in the far north all have well-equipped marinas. The Gulf of Asinara is an up-and-coming sailing area in the northwest, with harbours at Castelsardo, Stintino and Alghero. The Sulcis coast around Sant'Antioco and Carloforte is particularly technically demanding due to the wind conditions.

WIND- & KITESURFING

The exposed coasts of the north are best suited to wind- and kitesurfing, particularly between Olbia and Castelsardo; the trendiest spot is *Porto Pollo* near Palau, with its hip beach bars. But the flat beaches of the west also offer good conditions at Stintino and Alghero and around the Sinis Peninsula (Capo Mannu, Putzu Idu, Funtana Meiga). Top spots in the south are Torre Chia and Capo Carbonara near Villasimius. Kitesurfers in the know head to the otherwise unattractive beach at Porto Botte, opposite the Isola Sant'Antioco.

INSIDER TIP
Wind and waves all to yourself

The best kitesurfing school in the south is *Kite Generation (tel. 32 75 37 60 16 | kitegeneration.com),* which runs kitesurfing practice sessions, camps and competitions, plus courses in windsurfing and paddle-boarding.

Walking in the Supramonte is a multi-sensory experience

REGIONAL OVERVIEW

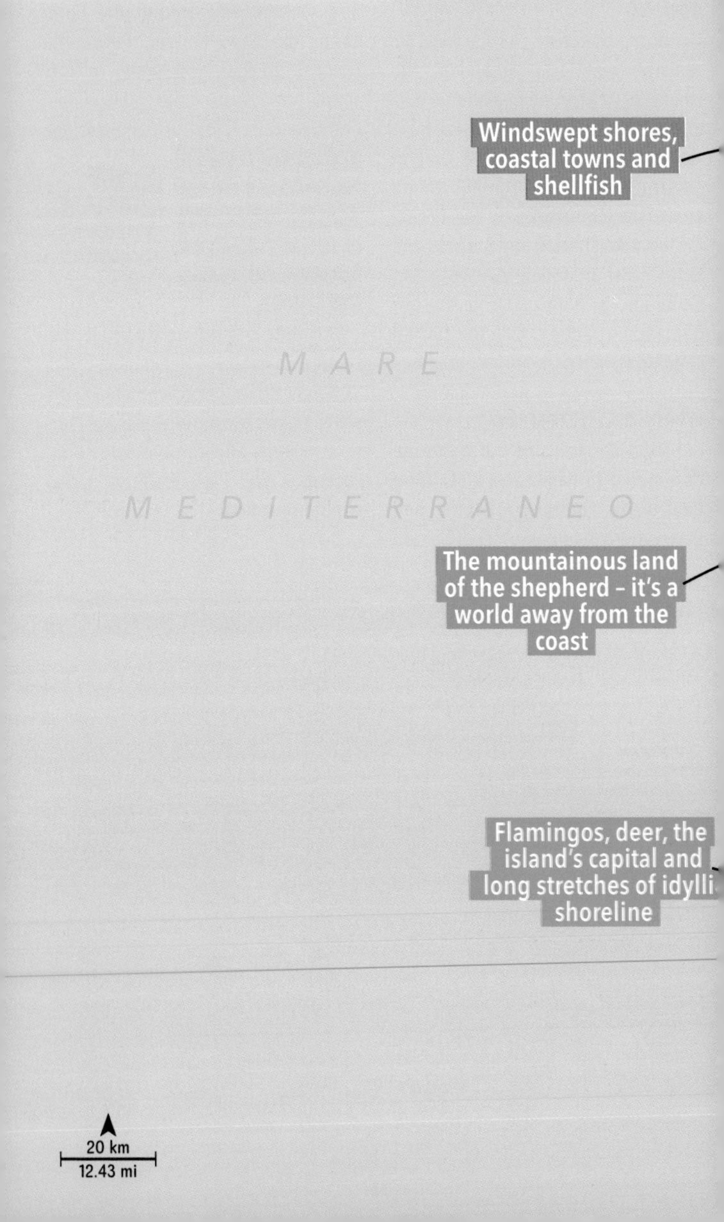

Windswept shores, coastal towns and shellfish

MARE

MEDITERRANEO

The mountainous land of the shepherd – it's a world away from the coast

Flamingos, deer, the island's capital and long stretches of idylli shoreline

20 km
12.43 mi

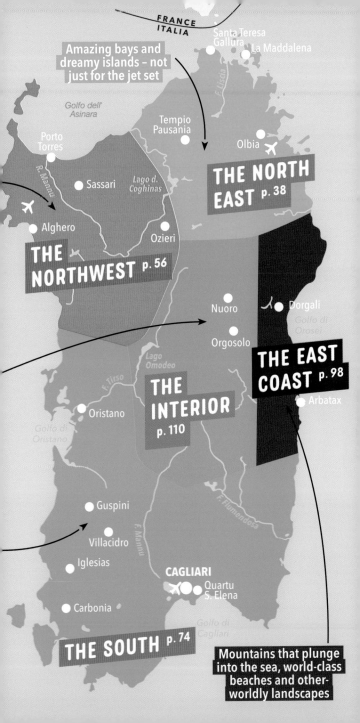

FRANCE
ITALIA

Santa Teresa
Gallura
La Maddalena

Amazing bays and
dreamy islands – not
just for the jet set

Golfo dell'
Asinara

Tempio
Pausania

Olbia ✈

Porto
Torres

R. Mannu

Sassari

Lago d.
Coghinas

**THE NORTH
EAST** p. 38

✈

Alghero

Ozieri

**THE
NORTHWEST** p. 56

Nuoro

Dorgali

Golfo di
Orosei

Orgosolo

Lago
Omodeo

**THE EAST
COAST** p. 98

F. Tirso

**THE
INTERIOR**
p. 110

Oristano

Arbatax

Golfo di
Oristano

Guspini

F. Flumendosa

Villacidro

F. Mannu

Iglesias

CAGLIARI

✈ Quartu
S. Elena

Carbonia

Golfo di
Cagliari

THE SOUTH p. 74

Mountains that plunge
into the sea, world-class
beaches and other-
worldly landscapes

THE NORTHEAST

The once-barren landscape of Gallura and the Costa Smeralda is where the straw-coloured Vermentino white wine is cultivated, and where everyone from billionaires to budget holiday-makers comes for a break. It's a feast for the senses: bright blue seas, romantic coves, bizarre granite outcrops and picturesque cork trees, surrounded by fragrant maquis.

It's no wonder that this corner of Sardinia bewitches all who come here: from the super-rich villa- and yacht-owners; to the parade of

Turquoise sea and granite outcrops at Capo Testa

celebrities from film, politics, music and showbusiness; to the average Joe, who can find holiday deals in the area south of Olbia.

Summer nights are long in San Teodoro, where villa guests and campers alike party until the small hours in exclusive clubs and simple beach bars. Yet those who drive for just a few short minutes away from the coast will find themselves in the real Gallura, a cherished cultural landscape that is slowly and cautiously opening up its treasures to tourism.

FRANCE

ITALIA

MARE

MEDITERRANEO

La Marmorata

Capo Testa ★ 12

Santa Teresa Gallura
p. 54

Frazione Ruoni

Conca Verde

Porto Pozzo /
Lu Puzzu

Porto Pollo 11
Lu Palau/Palau

25 km, 30 mins

Rena Majore/
Rena Majori

200

Vignola Mare

Bassacutena

133

Aglientu

13 Costa Paradiso
Spiaggia Li Cossi

8 Luogosanto

Coddu Vecchiu 7
La Prisgiona 7

Lago del
Liscia

90 km, 90 mins

Olivastri
Millenari 4

La Trinità e Vignola/
Trinità d'Agultu e Vignola

Sant'Antoni di Gaddura/
Sant'Antonio di Gallura

5 Aggius

Luris/Luras

Caragnani/
Calangianus

5 Tempio Pausania ★

Bultiggjata/
Bortigiadas

Telti

5 Monte Limbara ★

Erula

Belchidda/
Berchidda

Monte/
Monti

Tula

Oscheri/Oschiri

MARCO POLO HIGHLIGHTS

★ **CAPO CODA CAVALLO**
A view, a beach and lots of flamingos: what else could you want? ➤ p. 43

★ **TEMPIO PAUSANIA**
This granite mountain town has a refreshing climate and a unique atmosphere ➤ p. 46

★ **MONTE LIMBARA**
Ascend the highest peak in the region to have the north of the island spread out before you on a clear day ➤ p. 46

★ **CAPRERA**
Bays, beaches and Garibaldi: combine nature and culture on a road trip around this unique island ➤ p. 53

★ **CAPO TESTA**
At the northern tip of Sardinia, immense towers of granite form impressive sculptures ➤ p. 55

Maddalena
▲ p. 51   Cala Coticcio

10 **Caprera** ★

9 Capo d'Orso

Baja Sardinia   ○ Porto Cervo

Poltu
Quatu

○ Cannigione   **Grande Pevero**

Costa Smeralda
p. 48

6 Arzachena   Capriccioli

40 km · 50 mins

Cugnana Verde ○

3 **Porto Rotondo**

2 **Golfo Aranci**

○ Pittulongu

Olbia
p. 43

30 km · 40 mins

Murta Maria ○

1 **Tavolara**

Poltu San Pàulu/
○ Porto San Paolo

Vacciledди ○

○ 729 Enas

○ Loiri

Trudda ○   ○ Castagna

131

Cala Brandinchi

Capo Coda Cavallo ★

*Mare
Tirreno*

○ Padru

San Teodoro
p. 42

▲

5 km
3.1 mi

Sozza ○   131

SAN TEODORO

(⊞ G6) **The beaches to the south of Olbia can rightly be compared with those in the Caribbean, although here each beach is backed by a *pinete* – a shady pine grove that is characteristic of the region.** It is thanks to these beaches that the former fishing villages of San Teodoro and Budoni have become major tourist destinations. There aren't many large hotels; instead, accommodation is in holiday villages, apartments and campsites. San Teodoro (pop. 1,700) itself has long wide beaches and is one of the island's nightlife hotspots.

EATING & DRINKING

IL GIARDINACCIO
Excellent, beautifully presented food, a welcoming atmosphere and friendly service. *Daily | Via Sardegna 39 | tel. 07 84 86 56 78 | ristorante ilgiardinaccio.com | €€–€€€*

SPORT & ACTIVITIES

La Cinta beach is the location of the water-sports school, *Kitesurf San Teodoro (tel. 34 79 34 86 91 | kitesurf-santeodoro.it).* If you fancy flying above the sea, land and lagoons, climb aboard a microlight, piloted by Salvatore or Fritz from *Aviosuperficie*

Living the dream on Capo Coda Cavallo

San Teodoro (SS 125 Km293 | tel. 34 73 70 15 65 | santeodoroulm.it).

For a peaceful walk away from the hustle and bustle, make your way to Padru and follow the sign marked *Monte Nieddu;* leave the car at the end of the road and continue on a footpath. You will reach a high ridge that can also be accessed from the district of Buddittogliu, south of San Teodoro: turn right into Via Aresula and follow this road as far as the forester's house. To avoid damaging the under-carriage, leave your car before you reach the steep uphill slope. The *Rio Pitrisconi* flows through this area, creating two pools that are perfect for a refreshing dip. You can even abseil down the waterfalls by joining a canyoning expedition with *Sardinia Trekking (sardiniatrekking.it).*

BEACHES

La Cinta is a 3-km spit of land that offers the ultimate in sun, sea and sand. But the epitome of a beach paradise is to be found on the ★ *Capo Coda Cavallo* peninsula to the north, where the idyllic ✱ *Cala Brandinchi* slopes gently towards the open sea – this really is one of the most beautiful beaches on the island. The wide bay of *Lu Impostu* is also gorgeous but is more exposed to the wind. You can reach both beaches from the same car park.

Pink flamingos can be seen year-round on the 🔊 *Salina Bamba* lagoon. Little known is the wonderful *Isuledda* sand bank south of San Teodoro. There are also beautiful strands, back by pine groves, to be found around *Budoni,* a

village that stretches along a single main street further to the south.

NIGHTLIFE

In high season, young Sardinians, visiting Italians and every other night owl go out on the town in San Teodoro. The evening starts either at *Bal Harbour (Via Stintino | balharbour.it),* an outdoor cocktail bar and restaurant around a swimming pool, or in the lounge garden of the *Ambra Day (Via Sardegna 20 | ambraday.it).* Afterwards, the party continues at *Ambra Night (Via Cala d'Ambra 1 | FB: AmbraNightOfficial)* or in the *Luna Glam Club (Stirritoggiu | lunaglamclub.com).* If you prefer a more relaxed, eclectic vibe, then the *Coclearia* night market *(July–early Sept daily from 8pm)* is the perfect place for shopping, drinking, seeing and being seen.

OLBIA

(▢ F5) **For most of the holiday-makers travelling to Sardinia by plane or ferry, this port town (pop. 60,000) is likely to be their first encounter with the island.**

These days, Olbia is the island's main tourist centre, although the town reverts to being a provincial backwater in winter.

The historic centre is small but appealing – perfect for killing time before your departure flight, buying a last-minute souvenir, or if you just want to hang out in an urban setting after the rural tranquility of the rest of the island. 🐗 Your best bet is to park at the harbour (Molo Brin) and walk from there into town; most of the central area is restricted to residents-only parking, although the signs that tell you this *(ZTL – Zona a Traffico Limitato)* are hard to see.

INSIDER TIP
Don't get a parking ticket!

EATING & DRINKING

ANTICA TRATTORIA

Small, comfortable restaurant in the centre, with Sardinian specialities and fresh fish. *Closed Sun, also Mon in winter | Via delle Terme 1 | tel. 0 78 92 40 53 | anticatrattoriaolbia. com | €€*

TRATTORIA ROSSI

Signori Rossi's restaurant is on Pittulongu beach with views of Tavolara island. Tuck into shellfish, simple anchovies or "just" a bowl of pasta – it doesn't get more Mediterranean than this. And if you have any doubts about the view, you can check it out in advance via the live webcam on the website. *Daily | tel. 0 78 93 90 42 | trattoriarossi.it | €€–€€€*

BEACHES

A municipal bus runs to *Pittulongu* beach, following the coastal road towards Golfo Aranci. The beach has a lido, restaurants, bars and sports gear for hire. Further on, a gravel track on the right leads down to *Cala Sassari*, a bay with a super view of Tavolara island and a trendy beach bar – *Fino Beach* (finobeach.it). Beautiful and popular bays south of Olbia include *Porto Istana* and *Porto della Tavena*.

Capo Ceraso remains relatively isolated. From the gravel road, a few dead-end tracks lead to small coves. Right at the end of the cape, a small path signposted "Stazione di Vedetta/ Ceraso" leads to a lookout spot. The view is well worth the 20-minute scramble to get there, especially at sunset.

INSIDER TIP
A romantic panorama

AROUND OLBIA

① TAVOLARA

15 mins by boat from Porto San Paolo, which is 15km southeast of Olbia
This limestone island, 5km long and 565m high, rises like the back of a sea monster almost vertically out of the sea. When the sea is calm, excursion boats make the crossing from Porto San Paolo south of Olbia (tavolaratraghetti.it). There are stunning beaches and two restaurants on the island, but most of it is a military exclusion zone. The crossing is particularly worthwhile for experienced rock climbers with kit; walkers with a head for heights can get about halfway up after half an hour of scrambling – even from this point, the view is breathtaking. The paths up the mountain are

Tavolara rises 565m from the sea, but only experienced climbers can reach the top

hard to find: from the landing stage, follow the coast to the right until you reach two old lime kilns and a large holm oak tree. *⊞ G5*

2 GOLFO ARANCI

35 mins northeast of Olbia by regional train

Is Porto Cervo the place to see and be seen? Not any more. If you're after a bit of glamour, high-end shopping and luxury living, head to this little harbour town. Where, just a few years ago, the train ferries from the mainland were loaded up, now you can stroll along the redeveloped harbour promenade, ogling the jewellery, fashion and luxury brands. In the little *S'Incantu Wine Bar (daily | Via dei Caduti 38 | sincantuwinebar.business.site | €)* you'll be offered a plate of Sardinian snacks to accompany your glass of Vermentino.

And on the next corner, *La Capricciosa (daily | Via Cagliari 5 | tel. 34 20 40 08 77 | €-€€)* serves great fish, seafood or pizza on the terrace.

Adjoining Golfo Arancini to the east, *Capo Figari* is a nature reserve. The road runs alongside the railway tracks as far as a small car park, directly by the sea. If you're lucky, you may spot a couple of dolphins who seem to know exactly when the fish that are farmed here are due to be fed.

INSIDER TIP
Dolphin-watching for free

From here it's 15 minutes on foot to idyllic *Cala Moresca*. Behind the beach, a steep track snakes its way to the abandoned semaphore station on the top of the cape. *Mouflon*, a native breed of wild sheep, can be seen roaming the limestone cliffs and scrub up here. *⊞ G5*

3 PORTO ROTONDO
17km north of Olbia / 25 mins via Rudalza

The Italian aristocracy's answer to Porto Cervo lies on the Punta Volpe peninsula: Porto Rotondo attracts a wealthy and well-heeled clientele with beautiful hotels and villas, a yacht harbour and high-end shopping.

You don't have to be a fan of church architecture to visit the modern *San Lorenzo Church*; it's unusual wooden roof, which resembles the upside-down keel of a ship, and its Murano glass decorations are both well worth seeing.

The best-known beaches at Porto Rotondo are named after two celebrities: *Spiaggia Ira* (after Ira von Fürstenberg) and *Spiaggia Shirley Bassey,* which is located on the Punta Lada peninsula. There aren't many parking spaces at *Punta Volpe* beach – but from June to September holidaymakers in Porto Rotondo can make use of the free shuttle bus *Navetta Mare Mare*, which runs from the centre to all the beaches that have public access. Unsurprisingly, there is no public access to the beaches next to the giant villas belonging to long-term guest Silvio Berlusconi and his neighbour Vladimir Putin... *ⅢF5*

4 OLIVASTRI MILLENARI
40km west of Olbia / 45 mins by car on the SS 127 and SP 38, take the turning to "Diga Liscia"

Tucked away on the northern shore of the Lago di Liscia is a true wonder of nature: a group of three gigantic wild olive trees that are thousands of years old. They stand next to each other near the little country church of San Bartolomeo; all of them are healthy and green with new growth. The youngest is well over 1,000 years old; the one in the centre has survived for 2,500 years, and the awe-inspiring Methuselah, known as S'Ozzastru, is an incredible 4,000 to 4,500 years old. With a trunk diameter of 12m and a mighty crown, it is truly an emperor among trees. *Mon–Fri 10am–6.30pm | Ⅲ E-F5*

5 TEMPIO PAUSANIA, AGGIUS & MONTE LIMBARA
45km west of Olbia / 1 hr by car on the SS 127

Some 35km west, the mountains around ★ *Tempio Pausania* are lightly covered in cork oak trees. Thanks to its location at some 550m above sea level, the town of Tempio (pop. 14,000) enjoys a much fresher climate than the coast, even in summer. The locals value this feature of their town nearly as much as the cold, slightly mineral water that springs from the *Fonti di Rinaggiu* in the upper part of Tempio. The old town, built from pale granite, is a work of art – its cool beauty is slightly unsettling. If you take time to window-shop, don't miss the atelier of *Anna Grindi (Via Roma 34),* who makes unique clothes from cork. It's also worth seeking out the somewhat hidden *Trattoria La Gallurese (daily | Via Novara 2 | tel. 07 96 39 30 12 | €)* where Mamma Rosa has been casting her spell over the kitchen since 1976. Her magic can be tasted in traditional *zuppa gallurese* (similar to lasagne), but also in dishes such as lamb in white wine or sweet-and-sour pork.

The peak of the 1,359-m granite massif of ★ *Monte Limbara* is accessible by road. From here you can see the entire north of Sardinia and all the way to Corsica on a clear day. The US Airforce also appreciated this spot. Until 2008 they operated a radio intercepting station here with huge parabolic antennas. Great for a photo.

ER TIP
Eaves-dropping

Tempio's neighbouring village, *Aggius,* is famous for its unusually fine location below a massive rocky outcrop and for its traditional weaving. The engaging *Museo del Banditismo (Via* Pretura | May–Oct daily 10am–1pm and 3.30–6.30pm | museodiaggius.it) recounts, among other things, the story of the legendary bandit Bastiano Tansu, known as *"Il Muto di Gallura".* Excellent country cooking and own-label wine is on offer at the *Agriturismo Il Muto di Gallura (April–mid-Nov daily | Fraiga | tel. 0 79 62 05 59 | mutodigallura.com | €€).* You can walk off the calories by following the path behind the farm, which leads past the stables and through a cork oak forest. Follow the signs marked "Laghetto" as far as the small Santa Degna park with its little lake. After your exertions you'll have worked up an appetite for dessert. *E5*

Yacht owners moor up in Porto Rotonda

COSTA SMERALDA

(F4–5) **Mother Nature created a magnificent natural landscape of pink and rust-coloured stone, fine sand and outlandish rock formations around the Costa Smeralda and Baia Sardinia. Thanks to the skill and self-restraint of the architects – or rather, strict building regulations – hotels, villas and marinas have been built here without deforming and destroying the coast.**

It was in 1960 that the Aga Khan, billionaire and Imam of the Nizari Ismailis, "discovered" this undeveloped coastline and created a paradise holiday retreat for the international jet set. Horticultural design and generous irrigation were used to subtly enhance the natural environment. Architects based the buildings on the traditional fishing villages and farmhouses of the Mediterranean to create a neo-Sardinian style. Even after 60 years, hotels such as Cala di Volpe, Pitrizza and Romazzino are proof of the long-term vision of the original designs.

SIGHTSEEING

PORTO CERVO

Porto Cervo was created from scratch at the heart of the Costa Smeralda as a marina and meeting point for the rich and famous. The *piazzetta* is surrounded by exclusive bars, shops and boutiques, but there's also a 🐗 church, *Stella Maris*, built in the typical Costa Smeralda style that houses a painting by El Greco. The new *Promenade du Port* shopping complex has every essential imaginable, from personal shoppers to fashion for pets, complete with Swarovski crystals. The high point of any stroll is the parade of luxury yachts at the adjoining Porto Vecchio and the exclusive Yacht Club Costa Smeralda at the marina.

EATING & DRINKING

FRATI ROSSI

This local restaurant hasn't let its lofty position above the Gulf of Pevero go to its head. The menu features seafood and Sardinian specialities and the outside tables have a view of the sea. It's a bit hidden away in the Pantogia residential development on the road between Abbiadori and Porto Cervo. *Daily | tel. 0 78 91 87 64 86 | ristorantefratirossi.com | €€–€€€*

IL VECCHIO MULINO

This is a reliably good restaurant close to Arzachena. Prices are fair, and it's open 364 days of the year. *Daily | Moro district | SS 125 Km339 | tel. 0 78 98 19 43 | €€*

SHOPPING

A *craft market* is held every Thursday morning from May to October in the appealing granite village of San Pantaleo. Fine fabrics and handmade ceramics can be found every Friday morning in the Sopravento district, at the *Mercato di Porto Cervo*. There are also *weekly markets* in Arzachena

Porto Cervo typifies the neo-Sardinian architecture of the Costa Smeralda

(Wednesday) and Cannigione (Monday) – the latter sells fresh fish.

SPORT & ACTIVITIES

AQUADREAM

Heaven for kids near Baia Sardinia. There are numerous slides and a "Kamikazi" twister, on which your offspring will accelerate up to 90kmh. Thank goodness you can recover from the excitement in an inflatable on the "Relax River". *Mid-June–early Sept. Daily 10.30am–6pm | aquadream.it*

DOLPHIN WATCHING

DER TIP
whale of a time!

In season, there are daily boat trips to see the dolphins in the underwater *Canyon di Caprera*. It's an unforgettable experience. The excursion lasts seven hours and costs 120 euros per person, including lunch on board

and snorkelling gear. If you're unlucky enough not to spot a dolphin, you'll get a 20 per cent refund. *Orso Diving | Poltu Quatu | tel. 34 80 64 18 25 | orsodiving.com*

BEACHES

For the ultimate Costa Smeralda experience, head to *Grande Pevero* beach, where you can watch the mega yachts without moving from your towel. To the south and east of Pevero, *Capriccioli* is a granite promontory with several small, beautiful and popular bays surrounded by dunes, broom bushes and granite rocks. Access to *La Celvia*, a gently curved sandy bay at the southern end of the peninsula, is through a residential development.

The Aga Khan's favourite beach is the *Spiaggia del Principe*, a romantic stretch of sand that extends between rocky cliffs near Romazzino; it's reached via a footpath (approx. 500m). You'll also need to walk to reach *Spiaggia Cala Granu* in a picture-perfect bay on Capo Ferro, north of Porto Cervo.

South of Hotel Cala di Volpe, turn left at the sign for *Liscia Ruja* onto a dusty potholed road to reach the longest beach on the Costa Smeralda – it's sometimes marketed as "Long Beach". There are several access points to this extensive stretch of sand, but you'll also find a footpath leading to smaller beaches, which you might well have all to yourself, even in high season.

INSIDER TIP
Private Beaches?

NIGHTLIFE

Flavio Briatore welcomes you to his exclusive nightclub, *Billionaire (billionairelife.com)* in Porto Cervo, where the name is a clue to the astronomic entrance fee.

Designer fashion and fancy cocktails are on show at *Just Cavalli Porto Cervo (justcavalliportocervo.com)*.

The sunset parties at the Sardinian branch of *Nikki Beach (nikkibeach. com)*, on the beach at Petra Ruja, attract an upper-class but unpretentious crowd.

Baia Sardinia is also in vogue: *Phi Beach (phibeach.com)*, with its outdoor club and restaurant, is the best place for a sundowner.

A long-time favourite is *Ritual (ritual. it)*, a nightclub built around the granite rocks to resemble castle ruins. Costa Smeralda visitors have been taking to the dance floor here for years.

AROUND COSTA SMERALDA

6 ARZACHENA

17km southwest of Porto Cervo / 20 mins by car on the SP 59 and SS 125

The entire Costa Smeralda (pop. 13,000) lies within the municipality of this once insignificant shepherd's village. The old town centre on the hill has a large *piazza* where the locals gather, and there are pleasant trattorie that are not overrun with tourists – in fact, despite its celebrated surroundings, Arzachena is not so very different from other Sardinian towns. From the centre, a side street leads to *Fungo*, a huge granite block that has been shaped into a giant mushroom by the wind and rain; there's a great view from here.

INSIDER TIP
Mushroom with a view

Few visitors make it to the well-preserved nuraghic temple of *Malchittu*, a 15-minute walk from town. To reach it, simply park next to the tourist office at the entrance to town, and follow the inconspicuous track up the hill. Heading north from Arzachena, be sure to stop off at the cute *Lu Beddu* winery *(on the left on the road towards Micalosu | lubeddu.it)*, where you can enjoy a glass of white, sparkling Vermentino and a piece of *pecorino* against an idyllic rural backdrop; Max and Federico are happy to talk about viticulture with guests. *F5*

7 LA PRISGIONA & CODDU VECCHIU

20km southwest of Porto Cervo / 25 mins via the SP 59 and SP 14

The most impressive nuraghe in this region is *La Prisgiona*; whose main tower is over 7-m high and dominates the surrounding hills. To reach it, head out of Arzachena towards Sant'Antonio di Gallura; after about 7km take the side road signposted "Siti Archeologici"; the nuraghe is right next to the road. Close by, surrounded by vineyards is the "giant tomb" of *Coddu Vecchiu*. *F5*

8 LUOGOSANTO

35km southwest of Porto Cervo / 35 mins via the SP 59 and SP 14

Surrounded by 22 religious sanctuaries, this small mountain village is a place of pilgrimage – hence its name, "holy place". A 15-minute walk on a well-signposted but steep path leads from the town to the ruins of the medieval *Castello di Balaiana*. A few steps away is the small, picturesque country chapel of *San Leonardo*. *E5*

PALAU & LA MADDALENA

(F4) **The islands of La Maddalena archipelago are the upper parts of a long-submerged land bridge between Sardinia and Corsica. The seven main islands, countless islets and the maritime area that surrounds them together constitute the**

A boardwalk leads down to the sea at Baia Trinità on La Maddalena

Arcipelago di La Maddalena national park *(www.lamaddalenapark.it)*. The only town, *La Maddalena* (pop. 14,000), is an airy picturesque place located on the island of the same name. Snorkelling fans will want to check out *Baia Trinità*, the most beautiful bay on La Maddalena, with dunes, rocks and a fascinating underwater environment.

On the mainland, 15 minutes away by boat, is the lively fishing port of *Palau* (pop. 4,100), which has bars, restaurants and fishermen's pubs. The magnificent granite formations on Capo d'Orso, the extensive, wildlife-rich maquis and some good swimming beaches have resulted in a rash of holiday homes being built around here.

It's different in *Porto Rafael*, where the luxury villas keep a low profile between the granite cliffs. From here you can also get the best view of the archipelago. Shortly before the end of the tarmacked main street through Porto Rafael, there's an abandoned hut on the left; directly behind it, a flight of steep steps leads up a few metres to the highest point on the peninsula.

INSIDER TIP
Island panorama

From the top you'll have the islands of La Maddalena and Spargi at your feet – what a view!

EATING & DRINKING

LA GRITTA

Located in Porto Faro, north of Palau, this restaurant has a terrace with a breathtaking view. Simona and Roberto serve up delicious mussels, fish and seafood, plus some wickedly tempting desserts. *Closed Wed, Nov-March | Porto Faro | tel. 07 89 70 80 45 | ristorantelagritta.it | €€€*

PIZZERIA IL MAESTRALE

Super pizza, steak and vegetarian dishes with a magnificent view over the sea to Corsica. And, unusually for Italy, they start serving dinner from 7pm. *Daily | Palau | Porto Pollo district | tel. 07 89 70 50 33 | maestrale-portopollo.com | €*

SHOPPING

VELERIA IL PONENTE

This trendy eco-business makes products out of canvas, recycled from discarded sails. The shop at Via Garibaldi 11 in the centre of La Maddalena sells jackets, skirts and bags

INSIDER TIP
Wearable sailcloth

– and each item is unique. *veleriailponente.it*

SPORT & ACTIVITIES

ISLAND EXCURSIONS

There are daily trips to the islets of La Maddalena archipelago from Palau and a few other ports; some include food on board and they all incorporate a stop for swimming. *Spargi*, the largest island after La Maddalena, has a few stone huts and a Saracen tower; *Santa Maria* boasts a beautiful sandy beach, while *Razzoli* is much more rugged. The pinkish red sand at *Budelli* can only be photographed from a distance.

Bear rock at Capo d'Orso, near Palau

AROUND PALAU

9 CAPO D'ORSO

6km east of Palau / 10 mins by car

It's well worth taking the short drive along the scenic road above Palau towards the cape. At the end of the road on the left is a path that leads 500m and up a few steps to the "bear" *(orso)*, a colossal rock in the shape of a bear that gives the cape its name. At the top, you can peek through the bear's legs at the view of Palau and the archipelago. However, the bear's shape is only really discernible from the ferry. *Easter–Oct 9am–30mins before sunset | ⊞ F4*

10 CAPRERA ★

15 mins by ferry from Palau to La Maddalena, then 4km east by bike or car to the causeway to Caprera

While La Maddalena is relatively barren and rocky, the neighbouring island of Caprera is completely different. Not only is it forested, but it has both sandy and pebbly beaches lapped by turquoise water on its southern shore.

A few hundred metres after the causeway on the right, a large information board shows the network of paths on the island.

An unusual sight awaits you at *Spiaggia del Relitto*: here, the blackened remains of an old coal ship that is gradually being eroded by the winter storms rise from the turquoise water like a dinosaur skeleton. More hidden beaches, such as *Cala Serena* and *Cala Napoletana*, can be reached by following the signposted paths. The best of the lot is ✈ *Cala Coticcio*, also known as Piccolo Tahiti due to its beauty. However, the attractiveness of this small cove is no secret, and it can become hopelessly overcrowded in the summer months.

The Italian national hero, war horse and womaniser Giuseppe Garibaldi settled on Caprera in 1855 and began assembling his 1,000 red-shirts for the conquest of Sicily and southern Italy. After his death in 1882, he was buried in a huge mausoleum in the garden of his former home, which is now a museum and national memorial known as *Compendio Garibaldino (for opening times, refer to the website | compendiogaribaldino.it).* 🗺 *F4*

11 PORTO POLLO
7km west of Palau / 10 mins via the SS 133

Even American windsurfing legend Robby Naish recognised that Porto Pollo is a perfect windsurfing spot. Today it's one of the most treasured locations in the whole of the Mediterranean for kite- and windsurfing. The surfer parties are equally legendary. 🗺 *F4*

SANTA TERESA GALLURA

(🗺 E4) **Only 12km of sea separate Corsica and Sardinia. Ferries cross the** *Bocche di Bonifacio* **several times a day from Santa Teresa to Bonifacio, whose luminous chalk cliffs provide a striking contrast to the backdrop of high, forested mountains on a clear day. There's no need to take a car for a day trip to the French island; the fortified town can be reached easily on foot from the ferry port.**

Santa Teresa (pop. 5,200) is a fishing port but also a popular holiday resort, with bars, restaurants and plenty of goings-on in July and August. It's no wonder: the beautiful beach of Rena Bianca is right next to the town, and there are even better bathing opportunities in the surrounding area, including at Capo Testa and Santa Reparata.

EATING & DRINKING

DA THOMAS
The locals' favourite restaurant is right in the centre, on a side road that leads to Capo Testa. There's always fresh fish on the menu, but you should also try the ravioli with sweet ricotta filling. *Daily | Via Valle d'Aosta 22 | tel. 34 96 92 96 13 | ristorantedathomas. com | €€-€€€*

S'ANDIRA
On the beach at Santa Reparata with fabulous views over the sea and Capo Testa: a great setting for seafood, fish or canapés with your sundowner. *May–Oct daily | Via Orsa Minore 1 | tel. 07 89 75 42 73 | sandira.it | €€-€€€*

BEACHES

The town beach is *Rena Bianca*, a fine sandy bay that stretches for 300m right below the town. You can swim with a view of La Maddalena Island at *Spiaggia Valle d'Erica*, a long sandy bay that incorporates individual small coves separated by granite boulders.

Or travel for 8km south of town on the SP 90 towards Vignola Mare to reach the beautiful, long sandy beach of *Rena Majore*, which features sand dunes and shady pine trees.

AROUND SANTA TERESA

12 CAPO TESTA ★ 🐷

30 mins west of Santa Teresa on the footpath "SentieroNatura"

It is a unique experience to walk among the granite boulders on the Capo Testa peninsula, which have been moulded by erosion into truly fantastical formations. Those in the *Valle della Luna* are especially spectacular. There are also a few secret beaches – but beware the constant wind, which blows for at least 200 days of the year. 🔲 *E4*

13 COSTA PARADISO

40km southwest of Santa Teresa / 40 mins by car on the SP 90

South of Santa Teresa are glorious bathing beaches and bays hidden between fabulous red cliffs and rocks, and often only accessible via dead-end tracks. *Cala Sarraina (access from the SP 90 at km36)*, with its intimate little beaches, is a mini paradise; while the shingle beach at *Cala Rossa (access from the SP 90 at the Ristorante Il Geranio)* is a dream in red, yellow, blue and green. Picture-perfect 🐷 *Spiaggia Li Cossi*, near the Costa Paradiso holiday resort, is only accessible on foot, but from the beach 🐷 🐵 Signor Stefano will take you by inflatable to the stunning shingle bay at Tinnari. 🔲 *D-E 4-5*

INSIDER TIP
Budget boat trip

The granite cliffs on Capo Testa have been eroded into bizarre formations

THE NORTHWEST

IDYLLIC SMALL TOWNS ON A WINDSWEPT COAST

In winter, the wind here is so strong that the trees are bent out of shape, cowering against the wide-open landscape of the north-west like broken broomsticks. The wind known as the *maestrale* (mistral) rushes unhindered from the south of France across 350km of sea, gathering strength before it hits Sardinia's north-west coast, creating both long beaches and windswept plateaux.

The majority of the coastline is uninhabited and barely accessible by land. Porto Torres has been an important harbour since Roman

Spiaggia Lazzaretto near Alghero

times, although it is now disfigured by petrochemical plants. From here, Spain is not much further away than the Italian mainland, a fact that is reflected in the Catalonian architecture and culture that characterises the town of Alghero. Inland are the barren plains of the Nurra and the deserted plateaux of the Planargia. The numerous nuraghi and fabulous Pisan country churches around Logudoro bear witness to the fertility of the land and the former wealth of the town's inhabitants.

THE NORTHWEST

Asinara ★ 9

☀ Spiaggia La Pelosa

Isthintini/
Stintino

9 Stintino

MARCO POLO HIGHLIGHTS

★ **CASTELSARDO**
Medieval coastal castle, set on a hill
high above the waves ➤ p. 60

★ **VALLE DEI NURAGHI**
The valley of the Bronze Age fortresses
➤ p. 64

★ **ALGHERO'S OLD TOWN**
Lobster, shrimp, mussels: this seafood
stronghold is strongly influenced by its
Catalan past ➤ p. 67

★ **ASINARA**
Have you ever seen white donkeys
roaming around a prison island? ➤ p. 71

★ **BOSA'S OLD TOWN**
Cobbled alleyways characterise this
small town on the River Temo ➤ p. 72

○ Palmadula
8 Argentiera

☀ Porto Ferro
Santa Maria
La Palma
Sella & Mosca Winery   5
                          5
                     Anghelu Ruj
Palmavera
Maristella ○ 6   ○ Fertilia
         6 Foresta Demaniale
           di Porto Conte
Grotta di Nettuno 7 7 Capo Caccia

Alghero Old Town ★ **Alghero**
p. 66

45 km, 60 mins

M A R E

M E D I T E R R A N E O

10 km
6.21 mi

Castelsardo's location is striking by day and by night

CASTELSARDO

(□□ D5) ★ This small coastal town (pop. 5,800) was founded in the 13th century as Castel Genovese – "Castle of the Genoese"; then it became Castel Aragonese after the conquerors from Spain, before finally becoming Castle of the Sardinians.

The names may have changed but the prospect of the fortified town, which sits atop a wave-lapped hill defying wind and weather, is the same as it's been for centuries. Narrow lanes and flights of steps mean the old town is reserved for pedestrians only; elderly residents like to sit outside their front doors watching the world go by, while local women weave bowls and baskets.

SIGHTSEEING

CATHEDRAL

The best place to appreciate Castelsardo's dramatic position and romantic surroundings is on the terrace of the *Cattedrale di Sant'Antonio Abate*. It is no accident that the church tower, with its pretty Majolica-tiled dome, is set apart from the church: originally it served as the watchtower for the defence of the settlement.

EATING & DRINKING

CORMORANO

Fish and seafood – the menu offers whatever is caught on the day. *Oct–May closed Mon | Via Colombo 5 | tel. 0 79 47 06 28 | ristoranteilcormorano. net | €€–€€€*

BEACHES

The best place for swimming locally is the beach at *Lu Bagnu*. You can also swim at *Valledoria* and *Badesi*, long beaches that are great for kitesurfing and leisurely strolls along the sand.

Baia delle Mimose is particularly beautiful: a large, isolated strand characterised by pretty vegetation.

INSIDER TIP
Blooming lovely

The flat expanses of fine sand backed by pine trees at *Marina di Sorso* and *Platamona* make these beaches perfect for children.

AROUND CASTELSARDO

1 ANGLONA

Sedini is 17km southeast of Castelsardo / 25 mins by car on the SS 134

Heading inland and off the beaten track, you'll enter the uplands of Anglona, a bare, rather unspectacular landscape of extensive plains, small villages and a few pretty country churches. Right at the beginning of the road towards Sedini is the famous *Roccia dell'Elefante*, a weathered trachyte rock with a discernible "trunk". The cavity inside is a prehistoric *domus de janas* burial site. Similar building techniques are in evidence in the village of *Sedini*, where houses and lock-ups have been hollowed out of the rocks.

A little further on, beyond Bulzi, a dead-end road leads east to the Pisan church of *San Pietro di Simbranos*; it's black and white zebra-style inlays look particularly striking in the deserted setting. From Martis, a dirt track leads to the remains of a petrified forest in the *Parco Paleobotanico*.

Cormorano: *spaghetti agli scampi*

On the return journey to the coast, take the SP 92 past the *Lago di Castel Doria* reservoir. The road runs below an old Genoese tower, which lords over the river valley with a grandiose view across the wide plain of Valledoria. From here, take a restorative break at the *Terme di Casteldoria* near Santa Maria Coghinas, where healing mineral water flows to the surface all year round. The spa offers a host of therapies, or you can 👥 🐂 head around the back of the unprepossessing spa building to create your own treatments – here you'll find the health-giving mud,

INSIDER TIP
DIY spa

which is allegedly effective against joint pain and inflammation, bubbling out of the ground. 📖 *D5–6*

SASSARI

(📖 *C6*) **First impressions of Sardinia's second-largest city are of a lively but slightly neglected student town, although there are still glimpses of the riches of times past.**

Sassari (pop. 128,000) was always a vibrant trading hub that enjoyed freedoms and privileges, even in times of the worst feudal rule, such as under the Spanish viceroys. The old town remains remarkably intact and has recently been revitalised, after years of depopulation. With its narrow lanes, many not accessible by car, and its light-coloured houses and small squares, it has something of a village atmosphere. The Corso Vittorio Emanuele II, the town's main shopping and pedestrian street, begins near the railway station and ends at the Piazza d'Italia, where the 19th-century state flexed its muscles with the construction of huge administrative buildings.

The facade of San Nicola cathedral in Sassari

SIGHTSEEING

SAN NICOLA CATHEDRAL
Construction started in the 14th century in Catalan Gothic style, which has been preserved inside. The cathedral's façade was redesigned in the 17th and 18th centuries in highly ornamental Spanish colonial Baroque. ⏱ *30 mins*

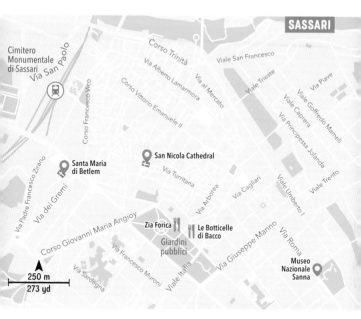

SASSARI

Map labels:
- Cimitero Monumentale di Sassari
- Via San Paolo
- Corso Trinità
- Viale San Francesco
- Via Alberto Lamarmora
- Via al Mercato
- Viale Trieste
- Corso Francesco Vico
- Corso Vittorio Emanuele II
- Via Piave
- Viale Goffredo Mameli
- Viale Caprera
- Via Principessa Jolanda
- San Nicola Cathedral
- Via Padre Francesco Zirano
- Santa Maria di Betlem
- Via dei Gremi
- Via Turritana
- Via Arborea
- Via Cagliari
- Viale Umberto I
- Viale Trento
- Corso Giovanni Maria Angioy
- Zia Forica
- Le Botticelle di Bacco
- Via Giuseppe Manno
- Via Roma
- Giardini pubblici
- Via Francesco Muroni
- Viale Italia
- Museo Nazionale Sanna
- Via Sardegna
- 250 m
- 273 yd

SANTA MARIA DI BETLEM

Once situated outside the city, the church is notable for its dome and unusually slender round tower. The Romanesque façade is still well preserved. Inside are nine enormous and colourful wooden candlesticks, decorated with tinsel, which are ceremoniously carried through the streets of the city during the *Candelieri* procession on 14 August – the eve of Ascension Day. ⊙ *30 mins*

MUSEO NAZIONALE SANNA

Of particular interest here is the archaeological section, which houses finds from all periods of Sardinian prehistory and early history, including small bronzes, menhirs and weapons. *Via Roma 64 | Tue–Sat 9am–7.30pm |* ⊙ *2 hrs*

EATING & DRINKING

While you're in Sassari, be sure to try *fainè!* It is a kind of giant pancake made from chickpea (gram) flour and olive oil that

INSIDER TIP
A Sassari snack

is laden with onions, sausage or mushrooms and baked in a wood-fired stove. You'll find a good version at ⬥ *Benito (closed Mon and at lunchtime | Via Sant'Apollinare 37a | €).*

LE BOTTICELLE DI BACCO

Fancy something other than an Aperol Spritz? High-quality wines are served as an aperitif at this wine bar to accompany first-class, local titbits. Evening meals are also available. *Daily | Via Torre Tonda 42 | tel. 34 73 43 37 46 | FB: LeBotticelleDiBacco | €–€€*

ZIA FORICA 🐖

Sassaresi of all stripes have been enjoying their lunch-break here for decades. Enter the barrel vaults of an old *palazzo* belonging to the university and be transported back 40 years: sparse furnishings, a short, simple menu, top-quality food and unbeatable prices. *Closed Sun | Corso Margherita di Savoia 39 | tel. 0 79 23 35 56 | €*

SHOPPING

Sassari is not a great shopping destination, although you can pick up a few pieces around *Piazza Azuni* and on *Corso Vittorio Emanuele II.*

NIGHTLIFE

There are pubs, bars and restaurants around the university. In the summer, the Sassaresi tend to spend their evenings on the coast near Alghero.

AROUND SASSARI

🖪 LOGUDORO: PISAN CHURCHES

Santissima Trinità di Saccargia is 17km southeast of Sassari / 20 mins by car on the E25 and SS 597

Situated in the middle of Rio Mascari valley, the church of *Santissima Trinità di Saccargia* is visible from afar. Its ornate façade and the portico count among the masterpieces of Pisan architecture. The interior frescoes are particularly noteworthy. *Ardara* lies a further 15km to the southeast on a hilltop with expansive views over the Logudoro plain. The small village is dominated by the "black cathedral" of *Santa Maria del Regno,* the coronation church of the Sardinian kings during the time of the *giudicati.* It was erected around 1100 by Tuscan master-builders. Thick columns with bulky leaf capitals divide the three naves. On entering, the eye is immediately drawn to the 16th-century altarpiece, which fills the entire height and breadth of the room and radiates gold and colours into the dark space. Another church that is worth a visit is the monastery church of *San Pietro di Sorres* (March–Oct Mon–Sat 9.30am, 10.15am, 11am, 11.45am, 3.30pm, 4.15pm, 5pm, 5.45pm, Sun 9.30am, noon, 3.30pm, 4.10pm and 4.40pm), enthroned on a hillside above Borutta. Marvel at the ornately decorated façade, with its colourful inlays and delicate friezes, before stepping inside to admire the ribbed vault ceiling and the bands of light limestone and black basalt on the columns.

🖪 VALLE DEI NURAGHI ★

Santu Antine is 42km southeast of Sassari / 30 mins by car on the fast SS 131

From San Pietro di Sorres, it's only a short hop to the *Valle dei Nuraghi* – there are very few other parts of the island where you'll find so many prehistoric sites clustered together in such close proximity. The imposing *nuraghe* of *Santu Antine* (daily 9am–5pm, Easter–Oct 9am–8pm) stands out clearly against a backdrop of stubble fields. The central tower rises 14.4m above the triangular fort, which was constructed between 1800 and 1450 BCE; embrasures and machicholations (opening through which rocks and burning objects could be dropped on attackers) are clearly visible. It's easy to get lost in the dark, labyrinthine corridors and stairways of the interior. One can only admire the skill of the builders who, without the aid of computers, mechanical machinery or cement, managed to manoeuvre huge stones into such perfect alignment that they are still standing more than 3,500 years later! The building techniques are explained in more detail by the tourist guides at the site. More than 30 Bronze Age forts are believed to have existed in this area, some of which can be seen in the distance.

The necropolis of *Sant'Andria Priu*

(*March–May daily 10am–1pm and 3–7pm, June–Oct 10am–7pm*) is located near Bonorva. The dead must have felt at home here, since the rock tombs are an authentic replication of domestic rock shelters at the time and are therefore particularly revealing for archaeologists. It is impressive how, 5,000 years ago, people were able to dig entire homes out of the rock with only the simplest tools. ⊞ *D6–7*

4 PORTO TORRES
23km northwest of Sassari / 20 mins by car on the E25 highway

Today, the image of Porto Torres (pop. 22,000) is defined by its petrochemical refinery and by the traffic that disgorges from the car ferries. But in Roman times, the city was an important trading harbour, as ancient artefacts and relics from this era testify. ⊞ *C6*

Romanesque frescoes in Santissima Trinità di Saccargia

ALGHERO

(🗺 B–C7) **Catalonia, crustaceans and coral have all shaped this coastal town (pop. 44, 000), but they are not the only reasons that this is an essential destination on your trip to Sardinia.**

Unless you're after cheap accommodation, ignore the new town with its identikit high-rises, half of which are hotels. Instead, set your SatNav to direct you to the large car park on Piazzale della Pace.

INSIDER TIP
Hassle-free parking

From there it's a short hop to the old town, which sits on a promontory ringed by imposing fortifications that protect slender church towers and colourfully glazed ceramic domes. Behind it, a wide bay opens up and, far out to sea, the horizon is delineated by the massive cliffs of the Capo Caccia peninsula. Beautiful *Lido di Alghero* begins in the town and continues for 6km as a strip of white sand edged by the rich green *pineta* as far as the neighbouring resort of Fertilia.

Spanish troops conquered the city in 1354 after a long siege. From then on the Catalans enjoyed many privileges that helped "Alguer" to become Sardinia's second-most important harbour and trading centre after Calgiari. The mighty bastions that protected the town against attack from the sea were never breached. The Catalan past is still very much in evidence in the town centre, and public funding aims to keep Catalan culture alive, but Italian is now

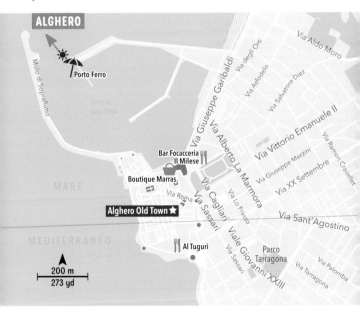

Experience Catalan culture in the streets and squares of Alghero

the dominant language on the streets - even in the old town.

The largesse of the sea dominates the cuisine in Alghero, with lobster, shrimp and mussels available on every menu. But the sea is no longer a rich source of coral because the Bosa and Alghero reefs are strictly protected. This means that any coral sold as jewellery in Alghero is either imported from Southeast Asia or is artificial.

SIGHTSEEING

OLD TOWN ★

You don't need a formal plan to enjoy a circuit of the city walls with a view of the harbour and Capo Caccia. As you wander aimlessly along the narrow cobbled streets, across the smooth paving of the *piazze* and past the ancient watchtowers, Alghero will start to get under your skin.

Entering the town through one of the city gates it quickly becomes apparent that Alghero is different. The street signs are bilingual, their names – Calle Mallorca and Calle Barcelona – testimonies to the town's Spanish-Catalan past. The façades of the churches and palaces, the beautiful stone ornamentation around windows and doors and the heavy vaulting are all reminiscent of the Gothic style of architecture in northern Spain. The most impressive example is the cloisters and church of *San Francesco* – an oasis of quiet in the heart of the old town. ⏱ *2–3 hrs, including a circuit of the bastions*

EATING & DRINKING

AL TUGURI

Traditional gourmet restaurant serving creative local cuisine from the sea and the land. The dining room is small, so it is a good idea to make a reservation. *Closed Sun | Via Majorca 113 | tel. 0 79 97 67 72 | altuguri.it | €€–€€€*

Sella & Mosca is the best-known Sardinian winery, with an international reputation

BAR FOCACCERIA IL MILESE 🐷

Since 1971 this place has been serving the most delicious focaccia, laden with so many ingredients that the tables groan under the weight. Freshly prepared for each customer and costing just 2.80 euros, this popular snack could easily replace a full evening meal. The nearby bar serves ice cream, if you fancy dessert. *Wed–Mon 7am–1am | Via Garibaldi 11 | barmilese.it*

SHOPPING

BOUTIQUE MARRAS

Are you in need of a new summer dress? This tasteful boutique is run by Filippo, brother of the Sardinian star-designer Antonio Marras. Grab yourself a piece of Sardinian fashion! *Piazza Civica 9*

SPORT & ACTIVITIES

BOAT TRIPS & EXCURSIONS

Excursions to the Grotta di Nettuno and round trips both start from the harbour. Some operators also offer dolphin watching trips – but they can't guarantee you'll spot one.

BEACHES

The long sandy beach to the north of the old town is called *Lido San Giovanni;* the more northerly section with finer sand backed by pine trees is *Spiaggia di Maria Pia.* As well as organised sections of beach with sun loungers and parasols for hire, there's also 5km of open sand that can be reached by bus from town. West of Fertilia, the beaches of *Le Bombarde* and *Lazzaretto* are recommended for swimming.

North of Capo Caccia, there are a series of sandy beaches with dunes and dwarf palms – a species that only naturally occurs here and on the Sinis Peninsula. After that, the coast as far as the northwest tip of Capo del Falcone becomes so steep that it is practically inaccessible even from the sea. Dead-end roads lead to the isolated bays of *Torre del Porticciolo* and ✈ *Porto Ferro;* where you'll have only wild dunes and windy solitude for company – the perfect places to get away from it all!

NIGHTLIFE

Most of the action happens in the old town, in the bars and ice-cream parlours on *Piazza Sulis* and *Lungomare Colombo* as far as Torre San Giacomo. There are also two nightclubs on the SS 127 road out of town: old-school *Il Ruscello (https://il-ruscello.business.*

site) and more-happening *Maden (madenalghero.com)*.

AROUND ALGHERO

5 ANGHELU RUJU NECROPOLIS & THE SELLA & MOSCA WINERY
10km north of Alghero / 15 mins on the SP 42
With its 37 burial caves from the Ozieri culture (3400–2700 BCE) and the subsequent Bonnanaro culture, this necropolis *(March and Nov daily 10am–2pm, April and Oct 9am–6pm, May–Sept 9am–7pm)* is one of the largest and most important on the island. It is situated in the vineyard of the famous *Sella & Mosca* winery *(tel. 0 79 99 77 00 | sellaemosca.it)*, which has been producing wine – including an exquisite heavy liqueur wine known as Anghelu Ruju – for over 100 years. Tastings are available in the *Enoteca (9am 8pm Mon–Sat)*, with a cellar tour in the summer *(June–Sept 5.30pm Mon–Sat)*. ▥ B–C6

6 PALMAVERA & FORESTA DEMANIALE DI PORTO CONTE
10km to Palmavera, west of Alghero / 20 mins on the SP 55
The *nuraghi* complex of *Palmavera (Apr and Oct daily 9am–7pm, May–Sept 10am–7pm, Nov–March 10am–2pm |⏱ 1 hr)* is not only unusual for its location right on the coast, but also for the very careful way the stone has been worked. The complex had a strong

surrounding wall and a central edifice with two towers. The round hut at the entrance was probably used for council sessions, as suggested by a throne of sandstone and the stone bench running around it.

To the west, the deep bay of *Porto Conte* forms a wonderful natural harbour. The coast and its interior are protected as a natural park that incorporates the 🐎🐗 *Foresta Demaniale di Porto Conte (off the SP 55 | April–Oct daily 9am–6pm, Nov–March Mon–Fri 9am–3pm, Sat/Sun 9am–5pm)*. This wilderness area is ideal for hiking and mountain biking. Don't be surprised if you see an untended horse during your explorations: the forest is home to wild ponies, albino donkeys and fallow deer. *B7*

INSIDER TIP
Take a walk on the wild side

🔳 CAPO CACCIA & GROTTA DI NETTUNO
25km west of Alghero / 40 mins on the SP 55

Beyond Fertilia, the coast changes character: dramatic limestone cliffs drop right down to the shoreline, rising softly at first, then turning into a sheer rock wall at *Capo Caccia* that rises vertically from the sea to heights of 300m. En route to the Capo Caccia lighthouse, the road begins to rise, offering an overwhelming view of the wild coast. It finishes at the car park above the *Grotta di Nettuno (April–mid-Sept daily 9am–7pm, mid-Sept–Oct 9am–6pm, Nov–March 10am–3pm; closed in rough weather – enquire at the tourist office in Alghero*

before visiting, tel. 0 79 97 90 54). To reach the cave, you either have to descend the 652 steps from the car park or visit by boat from Alghero or Porto Conte. It is one the largest and most beautiful sea grottoes in Italy. ⏱ *1½ hrs | B7*

🔳 ARGENTIERA
40km northwest of Alghero / 45 mins on the SP 42 and SP 18

To reach the abandoned Argentiera silvermines, head north via the small settlement of Palmadula, through reclaimed former marshes and the gentle hills of the Nurra. Today it looks like the filmset for an old spaghetti western, but in the 19th century this was the stage for a real-life silver rush.

Although the methods for extracting the precious metal were more reliable than those used by the Romans and Punic settlers more than 2,000 years ago, most treasure hunters still suffered financial ruin. Depending on the swell, the small beach around the derelict loading port has some good diving. *B6*

🔳 STINTINO & ASINARA
55km to Stintino, north of Alghero / 55 mins on the SP 42 and SP 57

The tiny fishing village of *Stintino* (pop. 1,600) is in a picturesque location on a headland framed by two fishing harbours. Delicious seafood is served in the family-run *Hotel Silvestrino | Via Sassari 14 | tel. 0 79 52 30 07 | hotel-silvestrino.it | €*) in the village; the restaurant prepares whatever fresh fish the boats have caught that day. The main attraction near Stintino is the famous 🐾 *Spiaggia Pelosa* at Capo del Falcone – which will send your Instagram followers into raptures of envy. It's often used as the setting for adverts and fashion shoots, thanks to its unbelievable colours, but it also attracts crowds of people, even in low season.

Excursion boats make the crossing from Stintino to the island of ★ *Asinara*, which is a designated national park. Fishermen and shepherds lived here until 1884 when they were forcibly relocated to Stintino so that a much-feared high-security prison – Italy's own Alcatraz – could be built on the island. It is said that not even the Mafia bosses that were incarcerated here ever managed a successful break-out – the only person to escape was a Sardinian bandit with the help of his wife. The prison's sombre remains are

not the only reason to visit Asinara: the island also offers pristine natural surroundings, idyllic swimming coves and, famously, wild white donkeys that roam free here. Asinara can be visited from Stintino and Porto Torres *(delcomar.it)* either on a solo trip or as part of a guided tour by foot, bike, horse, bus or on the island's electric road-train. *Information and reservations: parcoasinara.org* | ⌁ B5

BOSA

(⌁ C8) **It looks as though the colourful little houses of Bosa (pop. 8,000) are scaling the hillside in order to sieze the old Genoese castle. The little town is medieval but lively, and you'll quickly be captivated by the**

If you can't face 652 steps, you can reach the Grotta di Nettuno by boat instead

charm of its buildings and their occupants.

Time may not have stood still here, but it seems to pass at the same leisurely pace as the River Temo, the island's only navigable river, which passes through the town.

SIGHTSEEING

OLD TOWN ★

Despite its old-fashioned pubs, weathered *palazzi* – almost all of which are built from local pink trachyte – and dark, vaulted wine bars, Bosa seems to host a *festa* nearly every weekend. Wind your way through the cobblestoned streets and stop off at the small artists' studios – with a bit of luck, someone will invite you in for a sip of sweet Malvasia wine. On the riverside you can watch the fishermen fixing their nets; on the opposite bank are the abandoned *Sas Conzas* tanneries, where you'll now find some eateries and a small tannery museum.

CASTELLO DEI MALASPINA

It's worth finding a route through the confusion of alleyways in the old town in order to climb up to the old Genoese castle and enjoy the great view. *April–June daily 10am–7pm, July/Aug 10am–7.30pm, Sept 10am–6pm, Oct 10am–5pm, March and Nov Mon–Fri 10am–1pm, Sat/Sun 10am–4pm, Dec–Feb Sat/Sun 10am–4pm | ⏱ 1 hr.*

SAN PIETRO EXTRAMUROS

From the *Ponte Vecchio* (old bridge), a road follows the Temo upstream away from town, past gardens full of flowers, to this Romanesque and (romantic!) church, dating from the 12th century. *Daily April–June 9.30am–12.30pm and 3.30–5.30pm, July/Aug 9.30am–12.30pm and 4–6pm, Sept 9.30am–12.30pm and 3–5pm, Oct 9.30am–12.30pm | ⏱ 20 mins*

EATING & DRINKING

MANNU

Seafood cuisine at really good prices – which is why it is also popular with locals. The *risotto al pescatore* is poetry on a plate! *Daily | Viale Alghero 28 | tel. 07 85 37 53 06 | mannuhotel.it | €€*

RICCARDO

Amateur fisherman and "slow food" aficionado Riccardo serves top-notch cuisine in this unassuming trattoria 10km south of Bosa in the village of Magomadas. Try the fish and seafood caught by the man himself, but don't ignore the meat dishes and, in autumn, the mushrooms. Definitely book ahead! *Closed Tue | Magomadas | Via Vittorio Emanuele 13 | tel. 0 78 53 56 31 | €*

BEACHES

The coast around Bosa has only a few beaches; *🐾 Bosa Marina, a* large beach with ochre-coloured sand, is one of the nicest and it has some appealing beach bars. *Spiaggia di Turas,* a little further south, has the same ochre-yellow sand. For a more unusual swim, head to the 🎭 natural pool known as *Cane Malu:* in the bare rocky coastline, west of the marina, nature has

INSIDER TIP
Dive in

Pastel-coloured houses and cobblestone streets characterise Bosa

created a protected basin in the limestone, complete with its own diving rock!

There are excellent diving opportunities along the coastal road to Alghero at the *Torre Argentina;* the coast boasts bizarre rock formations and bright colours; though diving can be risky here, even in a light swell.

AROUND BOSA

🔟 MACOMER

35km east of Bosa / 40 mins on the SS 129 bis

This rather unsightly town (pop. 10,000) was an important communicaton hub in ancient times. *Nuraghi* can be spotted on the high ground, as far as the eye can see. One of them even has its own motorway exit (but only if you're travelling towards Sassari). The best-preserved

tower is the Bronze Age *Santa Barbara nuraghe,* from where you have a perfect panorama of the region. Of particular interest are the *Sei Betili* menhirs, situated in the *Area Archeologica di Tamuli (daily 9.30am– 30 mins before sunset)* on the road to Santu Lussurgiu. These six mysterious conical stone structures face each other in two rows, and three of them have breast-like protuberances. The assumption, therefore, is that this is an arrangement of three female and three male figures – although the "male" menhirs have no discernible sexual characteristics. 🗺 *D8*

🔟 TRENINO VERDE

The narrow-gauge railway runs from Bosa Marina to Macomer – but only on Saturdays from the middle of June to the start of September. The scenic route includes numerous hairpin bends and affords fabulous views; the return journey is by shuttle bus. For further information and tickets, *visit treninoverde. com* or *esedrasardegna.it.* 🗺 *C–D8*

THE SOUTH

SUN-KISSED & STRESS-FREE

The south of Sardinia is different. Despite being the location of the island's buzzing capital, the population down here is famously chilled. And this attitude is wonderfully infectious - even the flamingos that loll around the lagoons on the edge of Cagliari seem to have picked it up. They have succeeded in securing themselves one of the shortest winter migration flights possible. It is just 180km from here to the coast of Africa

Cagliari's old town has a commanding position above the Campidano Plain

The climate reflects this proximity: it is markedly warmer off the south coast, so swimming is pleasant from May until November.

Today's tourists are not the first people to discover the joys of Sardinia's south. For centuries, people have invaded this region, attracted by the fertile Campidano Plain, the iron ore-rich area around Iglesias, as well as the plentiful fishing in Oristano. Each group has left its mark on the landscape, perhaps most notably in remote pre-historic standing stones, some of whose forms are unique to Sardinia.

THE SOUTH

Bosa

3
Monte Ferru

4 S'Archittu

Is Arutas

Sinis Peninsula ★
p. 78

131

Crabas/Cabra

1 Oristan

Golfo di Oristano

Terraba/Terralba

Costa Verde ★ **6**

Güspini/ Guspini

105 km, 90 mins

5 Capo Pecora

5 Buggerru

Grotta di San Giovann
7

Nebida **5**

Domusnova

Iglesias
p. 83

Gonnesa

S'Ortu Manr

Portoscuso

Carloforte

9 Carbonia

12 Isola di San Pietro ★

Nekropole Montessu
9

Santu Antiogu/ Sant'Antioco

MARE

11 Isola di Sant'Antioco

Golfo di Palmas

10
Porto Pino

MEDITERRANEO

SINIS PENINSULA

(□□ C9) ★ **West of the regional capital, Oristano, the uninhabited and rugged Sinis Peninsula extends out into the Mediterranean.**

The small brackish *lagunas* and ponds along its length often dry out in summer, but in winter they are home to thousands of flamingos who paddle in the ankle-deep water. Thanks to its rich diversity of flora, much of the coast around here is protected.

SIGHTSEEING

STAGNO DI CABRAS

This large lagoon is probably the best inland fishing spot on the island. You can almost pull out saltwater fish like eel and grey mullet with your bare hands. Sardinians are particularly keen on mullet for their roe, which they use to make *bottarga*. This local take on caviar, which was once the daily staple of fishermen here, is salted and dried and then cut into slices or grated over pasta.

Cabras may not be the most stunning place on Sardinia but it does have some of the island's best fish restaurants. It is not uncommon for Cagliarians to drive here for a fish dinner. Two of the many good options are *Zia Beledda (daily | Via Amsicora 43 | tel. 07 83 29 08 01 | €€)* and *Il Caminetto (closed Mon | Via Battisti 8 | tel. 0 78 33 91 13 92 | ristoranteilcaminetto cabras. com | €–€€)*. The main social focus for locals here is the sandy *Torre Grande* beach – whose lido effortlessly morphs from daytime swimming spot into late-night party location.

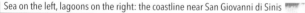

Sea on the left, lagoons on the right: the coastline near San Giovanni di Sinis

SAN SALVATORE

If the name San Salvatore conjures up an image in your head of a barren wasteland occasionally spiced up by pistol duels, you won't actually be that far off an image of this small hamlet in the middle of the Sardinian steppe. You could very easily be in Mexico … which is exactly what the producers of spaghetti westerns in the '60s thought. They used the hamlet (once a place of pilgrimage) as a film set. Pilgrims still come once a year to stay in the colourful bungalows, and the only real thing to see is the church (whose opening hours are far from regular). If you find it open, go down into the crypt find an ancient sacred well from the nuraghic period.

THARROS

At the end of the road to Capo San Marco, holiday cottages and fishermen's huts surround the early Christian church of *San Giovanni di Sinis*. The squat cottages are covered in reeds in order to make them look more "authentic" in this ancient coastal landscape. Further along the narrow spit, *Tharros (April/May and Oct daily 9am–6pm, June/July and Sept 9am–7pm, Aug 9am–8pm, Nov–March Tue–Sat 9am–5pm | tharros.sardegna. it),* the biggest Punic-Roman town on Sardinia, offers a more authentic vision of ancient settlement on this promontory. And what a town it was! Excavations have so far only revealed the centre but this gives a pretty good idea of how imposing this port town once was, with well-maintained houses, temples and baths. And the history does not end there. The crowning glory of the *Capo San Marco* is a monumental watchtower built by the Spanish in the 17th century.

BEACHES

The beaches of *Mari Ermi* and *Is Arutas* are well known across the island for their rice-like sand. What marks these beaches out is the idyllic contrast between the quartz crystals of their sand and the azure blue of the sea. Maimoni beach is much less well known than the others but no less beautiful. Even at the height of the season, you should be able to find a secluded spot along its length.

INSIDER TIP
Beautiful beaches without the crowds

The miniscule spherical grains of quartz make for a magical beach break; be careful though, taking sand off the beaches is strictly forbidden and can be punished with heavy fines.

AROUND SINIS PENINSULA

1 ORISTANO

8km southeast of Cabras / 15 mins on the SP 3, SP 1 and SP 56

The province's capital (pop. 32,000) sits on the edge of the Campidano Plain and is the most important city on Sardinia for both agriculture and the fishing industry. In the 14th century, Oristano was the capital of the Judicate (Province) of Arborea and it was around this time that the city experienced its boom period. Under Spanish rule, it went into decline and became the provincial town it is today. There are plenty of pretty corners to make a stroll around it worthwhile.

Begin inside the old city walls, as it is only within them that you get any sense of this as a living, even bustling place. The late medieval tower of *San Cristoforo* marks the entrance to the old town. The large *Piazza Eleonora d'Arborea* is named after a popular Sardinian hero, whose legend is celebrated across the island; the square has a large, imposing statue of her in its middle. At the *piazza*'s western edge lies the classical convent and church of *San Francesco*. And just a few metres further along the *Via Duomo*, the cathedral's spire towers out above the surrounding roofs. The depiction of the starry sky in its octagonal dome is the jewel of this building, constructed in 1195.

2 ABBASANTA PLATEAU

25km northeast from Cabras to Santa Cristina / 30 mins on the fast road

Most Sardinians only think of the Abbasanta as the point where three fast roads all called SS 131 converge. However, the plateau was a cradle of Sardinian culture and tradition, and the pilgrimage sites here are as impressive now as they were in the medieval period. Pilgrims to *Santa Cristina* today have it a lot easier than their forefathers. The archaeological site lies just off the main road and is kitted out with an espresso bar and restaurant. Its best-kept treasure is,

however, the wonderfully well-preserved underground holy spring, *Santa Cristina (daily 8.30am–1 hr before sunset | ⏱ 1½ hrs)*. There has been some kind of well here for over 3,000 years and not much has changed in its form since then. To reach it, you go down 25 steps: make sure to look up where the ceiling is a mirror image of the staircase. It's a superbly conceived Bronze Age geometric puzzle which must have depended on the most accurate measuring and cutting of the basalt imaginable. If you go past the olive trees, you will find yourself at the nuraghic tower and an early Christian church with small cells for pilgrims.

The imposing *Nuraghe Losa (daily 9am–1 hr before sunset | ⏱ 1 hr)*, with its 13-m-high tower, is one of the best-preserved nuraghic sites on the island. Don't miss the entrance. The site's access road is well hidden on the outside of a bend in the road coming off a bridge over the motorway.

Fordongianus and its red stone buildings was an important military town in the Roman period. The *Antiche Terme Romane (daily 9.30am–1pm and 3.30–7pm, in winter 3–5pm | forumtraiani.it)* down by the river are home to hot springs that reach 54°C. 🕮 *C–D 8–9*

3 MONTE FERRU

33km north from Cabras to Santu Lussurgiu / 40 mins by car via the SP 1 and SP 15

Cork oaks, wild olive trees, nuraghes and endless walls are the backdrop to a drive to *Santu Lussurgiu* along the

The entrance to the Santa Cristina holy spring

slopes of Monte Ferru, an extinct volcano. From any of the many viewpoints at the top of the village you will notice how the houses here were built right in the middle of an old volcanic crater.

TIP
Romantic waterfall!

This mountainous place's best kept secret is the well-hidden 😮 Cascata Sos Molinos. The small stream that runs through the villages continues for about 1km along a valley before cascading over a sheer drop into a lush, green gorge. To find it, keep an eye out for a small lay-by on the SP 15 towards Boncardo (after the bridge on the left side). Then walk down steps into the valley below.

The women of Santu Lussurgiu were still distilling home-made brandy in their cellars well into the 20th century. The *Distillerie Lussurgesi (Via delle Sorgenti 14 | distillerielussurgesi.it)* continues the tradition of producing spirits in the village with great success. Visitors are allowed to sample everything they produce, and they sell their whole range in small bottles, meaning you can take a few varieties home with you. If you have to drive, try a Mirto praline, which contains only small amounts of the brandy. An old palazzo in the heart of the village houses the best restaurant in the area: *Antica Dimora del Gruccione (closed for lunch | Via Obino 31 | tel. 07 83 55 20 35 | anticadimora.com | €€)*. It is not only the surroundings and excellent food that make this a worthwhile dining stop, its owner, Gabriella Belloni, and her two charming daughters are experts in sustainable, slow food cooking.

San Leonardo de Siete Fuentes is a popular spot among Sardinians during the height of the summer heat. It houses seven icy springs in the middle of a holm oak wood. The small *church* of San Leonardo is – partially thanks to its large Maltese cross – an unusual landmark for Sardinia.

The SP 19 winds its way through the dense oak forests on Monte Ferru for some distance towards Cuglieri. It is well worth making a 20-minute stop at the *Casteddu Etzu*. After a steep climb to the ruined castle, you will be met by the most magnificent view. *Cuglieri* is best known for its excellent olive oil. The fruits for this expensive product come from trees on the volcanic western slopes of Monte Ferru. *Azienda Peddio (Corso Umberto I 87 | oliopeddio.it)* sells cosmetic products made using the oil. ▥ *C–D8*

◪ S'ARCHITTU

20km north of Cabras / 25 mins by via the SP 8 and the SS 292

Santa Caterina di Pittinuri and *Torre del Pozzo* are two coastal villages whose charm partly comes from the fact that their best days are a few years behind them. The coast they sit on though has retained every ounce of its striking beauty. White chalk cliffs jut out of the sea in stunning formations. At sunset, when the landscape adopts a red hue, they look like lava streams flowing into the sea. This reaches its aesthetic peak at *S'Archittu*, where the sea's powerful waves have carved a perfect arch out of the cliff. The brave leap from the top of the arch into the sea below, while those who prefer slightly less hair-raising activities can rent kayaks and stand-up paddleboards on the beach. The seafood platters at *Centrale Marongiu (daily | Via Lungomare 32 | tel. 0 78 53 80 46 | €€)* are not to be missed – nor is the wonderful view from its terrace. ▥ *C9*

Perfect for pottering: Iglesias old town

IGLESIAS

(C12) **Whichever direction you come into Iglesias (pop. 27,000) from, you cannot miss the traces of the 3,000 years of mining, which made this small city the centre of Sardinian's metal industry.**

It all started with silver extraction and smelting, but this was quickly followed by lead, zinc and copper mining. Today the landscape around the town bears witness to this industrial past. There is a lot of industrial archaeological work going on here and newly restored mines, allow visitors to see what it looked like when the mining was in full swing (*www.parcogeominerario.eu*).

SIGHTSEEING

OLD TOWN

If *Iglesias* the name summons up images of Spain (and some of its more famous singers), you will not be far wrong. *Iglesias* means church in Spanish and the town spent a long time under Spanish rule – when many churches were built … The old town (some of its old walls and guard towers still exist) provides an interesting window into small town life. Lots of the buildings have ornate ironwork balconies – of the city's historic wealth. But this is not just a historically vibrant place, the narrow streets in the centre still buzz with life. The Romanesque *cathedral* and *Santa Maria di Valverde*, a mendicant order church just outside the walls, are both relics from the 13th

century. The latter is particularly interesting for its complete lack of decoration. A network of alleyways leads out of the Porta Sant'Antonio gate up towards the ruined *Castello Salvaterra*. On the hill opposite, another path takes you up to the pilgrims' church of *Nostra Signora del Buoncammino*.

MUSEO DELL'ARTE MINERARIA

Descendants of miners give lively historical introductions to mining and technology in this museum housed in an old mine. *Via Roma 47 | June–Aug Sat/Sun 6–8.30pm, outside these times register by calling tel. 07 81 35 00 37 | www.museoartemineraria.it |* ⊘ *1½ hrs.*

EATING & DRINKING

LOCANDA S'ANNINNIA

If you leave Marcella's place in Gonnesa (9km southwest of Iglesias) without having to relax your belt, you only have yourself to blame. Traditional, regional dishes of the highest quality. Even the *culurgiones* are home-made. *Closed Mon in winter | Gonnesa | Via Iglesias 107 | tel. 0 78 14 51 32 | sanninnia.it | €*

VILLA DI CHIESA

Sardinian and Italian cuisine right next to the medieval cathedral. Delicious pasta and fish, plus pizza in the evenings. *Closed Mon lunchtime in summer, all day Mon in winter | Piazza Municipio 9 | tel. 33 94 75 26 87 | FB: Ristorante Pizzeria Villa di Chiesa | €–€€*

AROUND IGLESIAS

5 NEBIDA, BUGGERRU & CAPO PECORA

38km from Iglesias to Buggerru / 55 mins by car via Nebida

You have to stop in *Nebida*! The short walk to the *Belvedere* takes you around the hill where lead and zinc were once mined. The view from the top of the old machinery is impressive, but to the north on the horizon is the jewel of this stop. With its striking elliptical form and sheer cliffs, the small island of *Pan di Zucchero* looks like a ski jump in the middle of the sea. With this view to enjoy, the slow service in *Al 906 Operaio (closed Mon)*, the small café/bar at the viewpoint, almost seems a blessing.

The rest of your journey to the north will be marked by the extreme steepness of the road here. At an incline of over 13% on a narrow road, you will need all your gear-shifting skills at the ready. Passing through the small bay of *Cala Domestica*, where abandoned port machinery reveals an industrial history, make sure to head up to the cliffs briefly to enjoy a great view. At the southern end of the beach, follow the path up to a defensive tower built by the Saracens. The view is so good that it makes you wonder if it was really about defence at all.

With a new marina and the renovation of the old *Galleria Henry* mine, the local authorities have made a largely successful attempt to turn the abandoned mine of *Buggerru* – with its vertical rockfaces, hacked away by generations of miners – into a tourist sight. Check the opening times online on the mayor's website (*comune.buggerru.ci.it*) before arriving.

Wind and frequent bouts of harsh weather on the *Capo Pecora* spit can make it an uninviting place to visit, but on a fine day a walk along the coast here to *Spiaggia delle Uova* is a must. This almost completely unknown beach is covered in large pebbles which have been formed into perfectly smooth egg shapes. A quick glance and you might think you were in a dinosaur's nest. *C11–12*

INSIDER TIP
Egg-citing pebbles

6 COSTA VERDE ★

90km from Iglesias to Torre dei Corsari / 2 hrs by car via Fluminimaggiore and Guspini

If you were looking to describe the "green coast" between Marina di Arbus and Capo Pecora in two adjectives, you'd find it hard to do better than "remote" and "empty". Its landscape contrasts between mile-long stretches of pristine white sand dunes and the scrubby, wild undergrowth behind them. A trip to this unique landscape is best begun in *Torre dei Corsari*, a small holiday resort next to Porto Palma, which is famous for its enormous orange dunes. As you carry on south, you will pass through the old holiday resort of *Funtanazza* which is now little more than Ghost-Town-on-Sea. Watch out here, the ruins of these 1950s buildings might be so striking

Abandoned zinc and lead works overlook the sea at Nebida

as to tempt you into them but they are also extremely dangerous.

Skip the sad resort of Marina di Arbus to focus on the real adventure along the dune path (in bad weather it sometimes closes to traffic). You start by crossing two fords where you'd better hope your car hire is insured to the hilt. After this baptism of fire, you will arrive in the more sedate surroundings of the *Piscinas Nature Reserve*. The beach here stretches for 1km and is flanked by sand dunes which can reach up to 300m in height. There is nothing to do here but get out of the car and frolic in the dunes and then cool off in the sea.

Head back inland by following the bumpy dirt track through the Riu Piscinas valley. You will pass a number of abandoned mining villages before you emerge at Ingurtosu. One place definitely worth visiting in this inland

section of the drive is the knife museum
🔪 *Museo del Coltello Sardo (Mon–Fri 9am–12pm and 4–8pm | Via Roma 15 | museodelcoltello.it)*. As well as learning about the history of knife production on the island, you can pick up a traditional, finely crafted shepherd's knife with a ram's horn handle. The museum's in-house knife-maker and artist, Paolo Pusceddu, will gladly show you the largest folding knife in the world, which weighs in at 295kg. *C11*

🐗 GROTTA DI SAN GIOVANNI 🐗
14km east of Iglesias / 15 mins on the fast road via Domusnovas

This 850-m-long tunnel, richly adorned with stalactites, begins just outside Domusnovas. It is hard to believe that cars were allowed through just a few years ago; now it is only open to pedestrians and cylclists. As you pass through the tunnel, you will be accompanied by the babbling mountain stream that runs its entire length. After 20 minutes trudging, you emerge into the light on the other side. Don't forget to bring a torch and a jumper. *C12*

8 S'ORTU MANNU

15km east of Iglesias / 20 mins by car via Villamassargia

The "Great Garden" on the SP 2 is a huge park with over 600 fine olive tree specimens mostly from the 14th and 16th centuries. Among them is Sa Reina, "the Queen", a 1,100-year-old monster whose trunk has a circumference of 16m. *C–D12*

9 CARBONIA & NECROPOLIS OF MONTESSU

25km from Iglesias to / 30 mins by car on the SP 85 and SP 2

Despite the closure of the mines, the geographical triangle formed by Iglesias, Portoscuso and Carbonia has remained an industrial area. *Carbonia* is a planned town designed in the Mussolini era and formally founded in 1938. The extraction of cheap lignite here has long since ceased. A little further to the southeast, near the town of Villaperuccio, is the fascinating but rarely visited ⚑ necropolis of *Montessu* (June–Sept daily 10am–8pm). There are 40 prehistoric graves here carved out of the mountains and spread over two hills. Using a network of paths, you can explore the whole area by yourself. The two royal graves are

> **INSIDER TIP**
> Take a stroll around an ancient cemetery

particularly impressive – they look like two huge faces staring each other down. *C–D 12–13*

10 PORTO PINO

50km south of Iglesias / 1 hr via Carbonia and Porto Botte

Porto Pino's sandy beach is simply sensational. It stretches for miles along the length of a bay, protected by a lagoon on one side, and its fine, white sand and many dunes make it look like a patch of desert by the sea. NATO practises desert war in a restricted area on Capo Teulada. However, in summer the soldiers retreat and the southeastern side of the bay is opened for visitors. The best car-parking option here is in the middle of the laguna – in the summer it dries out. Take the dusty road to the left just before the village to reach a decent spot to leave the car. *C13*

> **INSIDER TIP**
> Car parking in the desert

11 ISOLA DI SANT'ANTIOCO

40km south of Iglesias / 45 mins via Carbonia

Sant'Antioco is separated from the mainland by a narrow stretch of water and a series of different-sized lagoons. The narrow land bridge linking the two was built by the Romans, and takes you so seamlessly from one side to the other that you probably won't know at what point you have left Italy's second biggest island or arrived on its fourth biggest. The town of *Sant'Antioco* is a typical busy Mediterranean fishing port. Early in the morning, you can watch as the fishermen return to land in their small boats. You can even buy some of their catch – you won't find fresher fish anywhere.

There is a second fishing village at the island's northern tip. *Calasetta* was purpose-built for Ligurian settlers and seems to have barely moved with the times. The *Spiaggia Grande* is the island's most attractive beach. For particularly special sunsets, head across the island to the southwest's craggy cliffs. The small islands around Sant'Antioco are not called *Mangiabarche* ("shipeaters") without reason. More than a few sailors have come a cropper or run aground on them. *C13*

12 ISOLA DI SAN PIETRO ★

40 mins by ferry from Portovesme, 28km from Iglesias or 30 mins from Calasetta on Sant'Antioco

This small volcanic island is a world unto itself. Its inhabitants are Ligurians who left their northern Italian homeland hundreds of years ago to settle in north Africa. They successfully kept hold of their distinctive culture, cuisine and language while there before moving north to San Pietro in the 18th century.

The "capital" is called *Carloforte* and exudes all the charm you would expect from a fishing village. There are plenty of places to go for a swim along the imposing basalt cliffs.

The lighthouse at *Capo Sandalo* is around 12km west of *Carloforte* and the breathtaking views from the cliffs here can only be topped by a dip in the sea in the rocky bay of *Cala Fico*. However, no one ventures this way just for a swim. The island's unique cuisine is the reason tourists make the trip. Freshly caught tuna is the main event in most restaurants in Carloforte. Two very reliable places to try it are: *Tonno di Corsa (closed Mon | Via Marconi 47 | tel. 07 81 85 51 06 | tonnodicorsa.it | €€)* in the centre of the old town, and *Da Nicolo (May–Oct daily | Corso Cavour 32 | tel. 07 81 85 40 48 | ristorantedanicolo. com | €€–€€€)*.

Before getting back on the ferry, make sure to pick up a snack you can

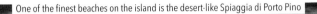
One of the finest beaches on the island is the desert-like Spiaggia di Porto Pino

only get on Carloforte: proper Ligurian focaccia. This fat-laced flatbread has been baked on the island since time immemorial and you can do a lot worse for it than *Da Gerolamo*, directly opposite the quay. ⫘ *B12–13*

CAGLIARI

(⫘ *E12*) ★ **Almost a third of Sardinia's total population (around 430,000 people) lives in its capital and the surrounding suburbs.**

The old town of Cagliari dominates its surroundings from atop a rocky plateau above the Campidano Plain, which – via a chain of lagoons and salt lakes – stretches out towards the Gulf of Cagliari in the distance. When the Western Phoenicians first came to Sardinia from North Africa 2,700 years ago, one of the first settlements they

WHERE TO START?

Following the signposts leading to "Centro/Via Roma" takes you to the harbour, with the historic centre stretching out beyond. An ideal starting point is the large secure car park behind the railway station, from where it's only a short walk to the **Via Roma** boulevard. From there, you can explore the maze of the Marina quarter, and head up to the grand Castello, which sits perfectly placed between the three historic neighbourhoods of Marina, Stampace and Villanova.

founded was "Karalis", with its prime location on a natural harbour.

You can still see some traces from that period in the city today. The Romans wasted no time in adapting what the Phoenicians had left behind, and in doing so revived the city. The Pisans and the Spanish were responsible for building the medieval castle quarter with its cathedral, and palaces for the archbishop, the viceroy and the island's noble families. The lower part of the city is dominated by baroque cupolas and grand façades. Today most residents can't be bothered to tramp up to the castle district, so most of the action takes place down below and in the districts of Stampace, Villanova and Marina.

SIGHTSEEING

CASTELLO

The old town and its castle sit squarely on the city's major hill. Not much has changed about the way you enter it in hundreds of years – choose one of the three city gates and ascend into the dark, narrow streets where washing flaps on lines and the smell of freshly made food emanates from every window … alongside the sound of daytime telly shows (we didn't say nothing had changed!). It is as close to the southern Italy you see in adverts for tomato sauce as you are ever likely to get. The two main defensive towers, the *Torre San Pancrazio* and the *Torre dell'Elefante*, with elephantine sculptures, are the works of highly skilled Pisan architects from the medieval period (although unlike the one in Pisa,

Believe it or not, the marble facade of Cagliari's cathedral dates from 1933

these towers don't lean). The top of the *Torre San Pancrazio* is still the highest point in the city, although it is in stiff competition with the gleaming white terrace of the *Bastione di Saint Remy* (a 19th-century addition) for the title of most beautiful place in the Old Town.

Sardinians call their whole capital *Casteddu* but for Cagliarians, this name only applies to the castle hill. The network of narrow streets is home to a small number of restaurants and the odd interesting shop. Some of the old *palazzi* have been transformed into expensive modern apartments blocks with stunning views. The Via Martini still exudes grandeur in both its breadth and the historical buildings, with the cathedral and bishop's palace at one end and the Torre San Pancrazio at the other, beyond the Piazza Indipendenza.

Getting up to the castle hill can be a sweat-inducing challenge. If you are in luck, at least one of the three well-hidden lifts will be in operation when you visit. Especially in the heat of a summer's day, there is no more sensible way to ascend to the old town. The lifts are all in the area just to the north of Piazza Yenne: the first is near Santa Chiara church on Piazza Yenne; the second is on Viale Regina Elena near the Bastione Saint Remy; and the third and final one is located at the bottom of Piazza Palazzo. You can also take bus no. 7 up to the castle. This bus route also serves as a pretty decent sightseeing tour through the Villanova district. And all of that for 1.30 euros.

INSIDER TIP
City buses for a sightseeing tour

SANTA MARIA CATHEDRAL

In the middle of the rabbit warren of narrow streets, a grand square opens up filled with palaces once occupied

CAGLIARI

Giardini Pubblici

Museo Archeologico Nazionale

Hortus Botanicus Karalitanus

Via Pola
Via Carloforte
Via Ospedale
Viale Luigi Merello
Via Ottone Bacaredda
Via Ozieri

Imperfetto — Santa Maria Cathedral

Gintilla
Via Caprera
Via Goffredo Mameli
Viale Trieste

Castello
Viale Regina Elena
Via Sidney Sonnino
Via Alghero

Viale La Plaia
Via Riva di Ponente
Via Sassari
Via Roma

Antica Cagliari

Parco delle Rimembranze
Via Logudoro
Viale Cimitero
Via Nuoro

Dal Corsaro

400 m
437 yd

Porto Interno

by the island's rulers. In between them, a white marble façade gleams out across the square. You'd think you were looking at a medieval building but this façade was in fact only added in 1933 when bits of the older frontage began to fall off. Inside, everything is as old as it looks – heavy, pompous baroque finery at its best. The many Spanish inscriptions around the interior are a helpful reminder (if you needed one) that this part of the world once belonged to a Spanish global empire. Make sure to go down into the crypt and inspects its 300 burial chambers. There are an incredible 600 different rose patterns chiselled into its vaulting. The marble Guglielmo pulpit at the cathedral's entrance is decorated with 12th-century relief sculptures depicting Jesus's life, which were originally intended for Pisa's cathedral. However, when Giovanni Pisano completed a new pulpit there in 1311, the old one was donated to Cagliari. *Mon–Sat 8am–1pm and 4–8pm, Sun 8am–1pm and 4.30–8.30pm | duomodicagliari.it | ⏱ 30 mins*

MUSEO ARCHEOLOGICO NAZIONALE

The most comprehensive collection of pre-Christian and ancient objects in Sardinia is housed in the new *Cittadella dei Musei* (which also boasts a gallery containing the best collection of Sardinian Renaissance art, and three other museums) at the highest point in the city. The museum leads you on a chronological journey through Sardinia's complex history.

Nuraghic culture takes up the most space and the bronze statuettes in this section are of particular note – they resemble models for a sci-fi film. In reality, their function was far more important – these metal soldiers, shepherds, animals and gods were used as votive offerings in graves or dropped into sacred wells. The exhibition of *Giganti di Mont'e Prama* has been long in the making as archaeologists sought to bring 38 3,000-year-old sandstone statues back to life from the 15,000 fragments they had found. Their success is plain to see, and this unique collection is now the museum's spectacular centrepiece. *Piazza Arsenale | Tue–Sun 9am-8pm | museoarcheocagliari.beniculturali.it*

HORTUS BOTANICUS KARALITANUS

Situated next to an amphitheatre to the west of the city centre, this botanical garden offers a very solid introduction to Sardinian (and Mediterranean) plant life. Under the shady protection of large pine and palm trees, the gardens thrive all year round. *Via Sant'Ignazio da Laconi | Tue–Sun 9am–6pm, winter 9am–2pm | sites.unica.it/hbk | ⊙ 1 hr.*

EATING & DRINKING

There is a wealth of excellent food to try in Cagliari. Every element of Sardinian cuisine is represented here, from the highly traditional to the very modern, and with ingredients from the mountaintops and the bottom of the sea. There are plenty of options in the Marina Quarter in both the Via Sardegna and the pedestrianised Corso Vittorio Emanuele II. In the summer when tourists tend to take up most of the space in the centre's restaurants, Cagliarians like to decamp to the district of Villanova around the three piazze of San Domenico, San Giacomo and Garibaldi where a small but exciting restaurant scene has developed.

INSIDER TIP
Eat with the Cagliarians

ANTICA CAGLIARI

This restaurant is something of a local institution serving classy fish dishes and fine wines, but don't miss out on the excellent pasta dishes like *strozzapreti* with sea urchins or *fregola* with langoustines. Reservation necessary. *Daily | Via Sardegna 49 | tel. 07 07 34 01 98 | anticacagliari.it | €€*

DAL CORSARO

This chic restaurant's dominant feature is its splendid art nouveau decor. The menu showcases an innovative approach to traditional Sardinian cooking. Presentation is everything here as the excellent chef, Stefano Deidda, strongly believes we eat with all our senses. Reservation necessary. *Closed Sun | Viale Regina Margherita 28 | tel. 0 70 66 43 18 | stefanodeidda.it | €€€*

GINTILLA

Virtually every trattoria will have at least a few decent vegetarian options but vegans may find life tough in Cagliari, the capital of an island in love with meat and cheese. As a result, this small, elegant restaurant sticks out from the crowd. Its food is experimental and delicious (and 100% organic). *Closed Mon | Corso Vittorio Emanuele II 210 | tel. 0 70 68 06 65 | gintilla. com | €€*

IMPERFETTO

Specialising in food from the mountains, this restaurant in the Castello District is run exclusively by women. Most of their ingredients are sourced from Barbagia, in the middle of the island. The cooking is exactly what you would get in the Nuoro Province … but for the fact the portions are much smaller. Try as much as you can – the food is superb. *Evenings only, closed*

Mon | Via dei Genovesi 111 | tel. 07 04 61 99 09 | €€

SHOPPING

Both of Cagliari's main shopping drags, the Via Garibaldi and the Via Manno, contain a broad but largely unexciting mix of international chains. However, tucked in among them are some more interesting old shops selling handmade clothes, shoes, hats and ties.

La Rinascente (Mon-Sat 9am-9pm Sun 10am-9pm) is a classic department store spread across four floors in the Via Roma. Alongside the usual department store fare, it stocks a lot of

Pillars, mosaics and temple remains at the Roman site of Nora

Italian design and fashion labels and local perfumes. Its greatest selling point though is its café on the top floor. The views from up here over the harbour only serve to enhance the flavour of their cappuccinos and cake. The huge covered market of *San Benedetto* is the place to pick up edible Sardinian specialities. It is also worth paying a visit to the city's gold- and silversmiths. They are focused in the Marina District *(Via Sardegna, Via Manno)* and around the castle.

BEACHES

The 10-km *Poetto* beach extends out along the coast beyond the Capo Sant'Elia peninsula (all city buses with P before the number will take you there). This beach is an archetype of traditional Italian beach life, with lots of lido options, swimming, bars and restaurants. Evening cocktails and late-night beach parties are a popular feature here, especially on the *Poetto di Quartu*, which is home to a number of trendy beach huts like *My Beach, Beer Beach* and *Jinny (jinnybeach.com)*.

NIGHTLIFE

Most of Cagliari's bars are grouped around the Piazza Yenne and the Corso Vittorio Emanuele II. Drinking carries on here well into the warm evenings. Those who want to keep going even later tend to head towards Poetto and its collection of clubs and late-night bars, like the disco in the *Lido (lidocagliari.com)* where the dance floor juts out over the sea.

AROUND CAGLIARI

13 COSTA DEL SUD
52km southwest from Cagliari to Torre di Chia / 1 hr by car on the SS 195

If you look in the right direction, the first 12km of this stretch of coastline could not be much more idyllic. Small promontories extending out into the wide, open sea, and narrows spits separating azure *lagunas* from the ocean beyond. Look in the wrong direction though and you won't see much beyond the chimneys of factories and power plants. However, once the Sulcis mountains rise up out of the cliffs, these eyesores no longer have any space and the coast reverts to its idyllic beauty.

The Roman-Phoenician port of *Nora (daily 10am–4.30pm, April–Sept 10am–6.30pm | sardegnaturismo.it)* sits on a very pretty, small peninsula near Pula. Its stunning array of temples, mosaics, columns and an extremely impressive ancient theatre are well worth visiting. At the tip of the peninsula a huge 16th-century Saracen tower sits on top of the Phoenician acropolis. From its top, you get an incredible view over the Gulf of Cagliari, the lagoon and the Nora. If you are ready for a swim, the *Spiaggia di Nora* sits invitingly close to the archaeological remains.

Santa Margherita di Pula is a small beach resort in a 5-km-long stretch of pine forest. With a wide selection of high-end villas and hotels, campsites and beach cabins, and its beautiful (empty) beaches as well as a rich offering of bars and amenities, it has everything you could ever need for a beach holiday.

However, if you think it can't possibly get any more beautiful, you need to get back in the car and head on to the ★ Torre di Chia. Both the beach by the tower and its near neighbour the ☀ Spiaggia Su Giudeu are so close to perfection they look like photos from a holiday brochure. But pictures can't show you everything. With dunes, the smell of rosemary from the undergrowth and oleander flowers, a Saracen tower in whose shade sit the remains of the Roman town of Bithia, beautiful coastal walks, and a remote island you can wade out too, we don't need to start listing superlatives. The facts should be enough to get you here.

If you are not quite done with coastal paradises by this point, head on to Cala Cipolla. From the car park there, it is a short walk to the fjord-like bay, which is not just a feast for the eyes but also one of Sardinia's best surfing spots. Following the path through the brushy undergrowth along the coast, it will not take long for you to reach the lighthouse Capo Spartivento, where you can play at being lighthouse keepers (or wealthy holidaymakers – it is now an expensive holiday let) and look out over the full length of this stretch of coast. Still have a bit of time? Then follow the bumpy coastal path for half an hour to the Spiaggia di Ferraglione. This remote beach is a wonderful spot to

swim from, so dive in. Apropos diving: the waters here are so clear and their wildlife is so diverse that it is definitely worth bringing a snorkel.

INSIDER TIP Dive in!

Back in the car, the road continues down the coast to the beach of ☀ Tueredda. This one is on almost all of the postcards you will have seen in Cagliari. The result is obvious – in the summer it will be so crowded as to lose much of its charm. Slightly further down the coast, there are less busy but no less pretty small bays and beaches. From them, a series of paths means you can walk down to Capo Spartivento and Capo Malfatano.

The deep bay of Porto di Teulada marks the point where the road leaves the coast and heads towards the large farming village of Teulada with its lush orange orchards. From here the rest of the way to Santandi is marked by a much more mountainous, rocky landscape. At roughly the halfway point, you should definitely make a stop at the Grotta Is Zuddas (look online for opening and tour times | grotteiszuddas.com | ⊙ 1 hr). Its dazzling stalagmites and stalactites are well worth seeing and the outdoor restaurant at its entrance offers decent food in a lovely setting.

Wine lovers must make sure they still have enough time to make a pilgrimage to the 🦅 Cantina Santadi (Via Cagliari 78 | tel. 07 81 95 01 27 | cantinadisantadi.it). Terre Brune wine, made using the Carignano grape, has become something of a global

INSIDER TIP Fine wine at a fine price

sensation and is still available at a reasonable price here. *D–E 13–14*

⓮ MONTE ARCOSU 🐾
32km west of Cagliari / 50 mins via the industrial sprawl around Stagno di Cagliari

West of the capital, the Sulcis mountains stretch out across the island. Remote and in many places inaccessible, much of the range has now been turned into a natural park. The WWF conservation area of *Monte Arcosu (weekends only, winter 9am–5pm, pre-registration and booking a tour are obligatory | tel. 32 98 31 57 54 | www.oasiwwfmontearcosu.)* is a park within this park. It was established to protect the *cervo sado*, Sardinia's endemic breed of small deer. There are also a series of walks around the edge of the reserve. *D12*

Flamingos on the Costa del Sud

⓯ SAN SPERATE
22km north of Cagliari / 25 mins on the SS 131 and the SP 4

You don't very often encounter street art in small villages, but then again not all villages are like San Sperate. As soon as you leave the high street, you will be greeted by colourful murals on every wall. Ever since 1968, people have been painting their houses in bright shades here. Not only that but there is also an excellent collection of sculptures by the village's native sculptor, Pinuccio Sciola, dotted around the streets. *E12*

VILLASIMIUS

(F13) ★ **Once little more than a village for sheep farmers, Villasimius has been transformed into a chic and modern resort (pop. 3,600) in recent years, with some of the best sea swimming in Italy.**

This development should probably come as no surprise given that the beaches around the village are not only extremely hard to beat aesthetically but also big enough to cope with large numbers of visitors without too much fighting over the best spots.

EATING & DRINKING

ARCADA
Fish and meat classics with a Sardinian twist, tip-top presentation and excellent, formal service. There are not many tables on the beautiful terrace so reserve early. *Daily | Via Umberto I*

13 | tel. 0 70 79 00 82 | FB: arcadacafe.
villasimius.1 | €€€

DA BARBARA

West of Villasimius near the village of Solanas, this restaurant has been a favourite among tourists and locals for generations thanks to its successful blending of excellent, fresh fish dishes with a relaxed, informal atmosphere. Reservation is an absolute must. *Out of season, closed Wed | 11km west | tel. 0 70 75 06 30 | €€*

BEACHES

There is no other town on Sardinia with such diversity when it comes to beaches. For picture-postcard beauty, *Porto Giunco* (turn off the road to Capo Carbonara just before the harbour) is hard to beat with its idyllic location with the sea on one side and lagoon on the other. *Punta Molentis* is a beautiful beach just off the SP 18 on the way to Costa Rei. It sits in a small bay with a granite rock desert behind it and a craggy island in the water. However, it is very popular so entry is restricted – you have to get there early. The pretty sandy bay in which the Hotel Cormoran sits is called *Campus* and is just off the SP 17 heading towards Cagliari. *Calo Pira* sweeps round in a gentle curve under steep cliffs and is just off the SP 18 towards Costa Rei.

Calo Sinzias is not just stunningly beautiful with its golden sand and perfect turquoise water, it also has a good number of beach bars which offer everything you need for proper lido service (at a full range of price points). Families will be best off at *Tamatete (lidotamatete.it)*, while hipsters are likely to enjoy *Is Fradis (isfradisbeachclub.com)*. For uncomplicated, excellent food with wonderful views, *Galeotto (FB: Il Galeotto Beach)* is hard to beat. *Maklas (maklas.it)* and its perfectly white furniture has served as beach wedding location for thousands of happy couples. The bay at *Monte Turnu* is perfect for nature lovers. *Scoglio di Peppino's* version of paradise includes juniper bushes, white sands and shallow, perfectly blue sea. It is also the border between Villasimius and Costa Rei.

AROUND VILLASIMIUS

16 COSTA REI

22km north of Villasimius / 30 mins on the coastal road

Apart from a large resort with countless cottages, a couple of apartment blocks and a few shops, the only thing here is the beach. Partly thanks to its excellent options for families, this is, however, one of the most popular holiday destinations on the island. Just north of the Capo Ferrato promontory, the apparently endless beaches of *Feraxi* and *Collostrai* stretch out into the distance.

Had enough of swimming and lying on the beach? Then go for a walk up to *Capo Ferrato*, where a very uneven path will take you to the old lighthouse. It does not get much more romantic. For a tougher walk, head to *Monte Ferru*. It will take about four hours to climb. Both walks are well signposted and start at the car park in Porto Pirastu.

A modest little herb dealer, *Erbe di Brai Loi (Feraxi | hof-brailoi.net)* is run by a Swiss man who has lived on the island for a long time. This is not a posh, touristy shop (it does not even have regular opening hours) but is a reliable source for excellent herbs, teas and seasonings.

INSIDER TIP
The best seasonal seasoning

From chilli to bay, rosemary or marjoram, he has everything and it is all organic. To reach the shop, drive to the farm gate and then beep your horn until someone opens up. The advantage of this informal arrangement: you pay a very fair price. *F-G12*

☑ MURAVERA

40km north of Villasimius / 45 mins via Olia Speciosa on SS 125 var

This village lies on the Flumendosa estuary and is surrounded by orange groves on all sides. Flat, windowless buildings give the place an other-worldly feel but real life carries on in the courtyards around which the buildings are built. It is a place filled with hidden wonders, including one of the best coastal views on the island from the old watchtower, *Torre Salinas*. To get there, park at the campsite of the same name, then scramble along a small, private path until you reach the tower. *F-G11*

☑ PARCO DEI SETTE FRATELLI ★

60km northwest of Villasimius / 1 hr 20 mins on the fast road towards Muravera and the SS 125 towards Burcei until you reach Km30.1

This national park is one of the best areas to walk and mountain bike on Sardinia. There are plenty of spots for picnics and the informative exhibition in the *Giardino Botanico di Maidopis (daily 7am-3pm, May-Sept 7am-6pm)* is a great introduction to Sardinia's flora.

More ambitious walkers should take route 812 to the stone towers of Perda sub'e Pari. The circuit (which also takes in a couple of summits in the Sette Fratelli) takes a whole day and has plenty of stunning views. Maps are available at the visitor centre and in the 🐦 *Museo del Cervo Sardo (Mon-Fri 9am-12pm, June8+9-Sept daily 9am-12pm, and 1-6pm)*, a museum devoted to the rare Sardinian deer of the same name. *F12*

Miles of sand on the Costa Rei

THE
EAST COAST

DEEP CANYONS & FANTASTIC BEACHES

The *Orientale Sarda*, national road SS 125 in the east of the island, is one of those roads that petrolheads dream about. And it has recently got even better with bypasses built around most of the villages along its length, meaning you can cruise through the mountains from Baunei to Dorgali for miles without even having to slow down for any pesky towns or villages!

Nonetheless even when high up in the mountains here, you are probably only an impassable canyon away from the coast where

Cala Luna may leave you lost for words

there are an array of some of the prettiest small coves and beaches on the island. Further south, you reach the flat plain around Tortoli, with its never-ending beaches. South of Bari Sardo, the rich red mountains and hills on the Capo Sferracavallo rise out of the sea like a bit of Mars on Earth.

North of Orosei, pine-lined coves nestle in between tall cliffs – the perfect landscape for an active holiday. You can walk, rock climb, sail and swim all in one day.

THE EAST COAST

MARCO POLO HIGHLIGHTS

★ **CALA GOLORITZÈ**
A good claim to be Europe's prettiest beach. Not to be missed. ➤ p. 103

★ **TRENINO VERDE**
This narrow-gauge railway takes visitors on spectacular rides through the mountains. The most beautiful stretches are those to Sadali and Gairo. ➤ p. 105

★ **GROTTA DI ISPINIGOLI**
Stalagmites and stalactites as far as you can see – one of which is about the size of a decent-sized house. ➤ p. 106

★ **GOLA GORROPU**
Sardinia's Grand Canyon reaches depths of over 200m despite being just a few feet across. ➤ p. 107

★ **CAPO COMINO**
Long, white, sandy beaches peppered with dramatic dunes. ➤ p. 109

131 dir

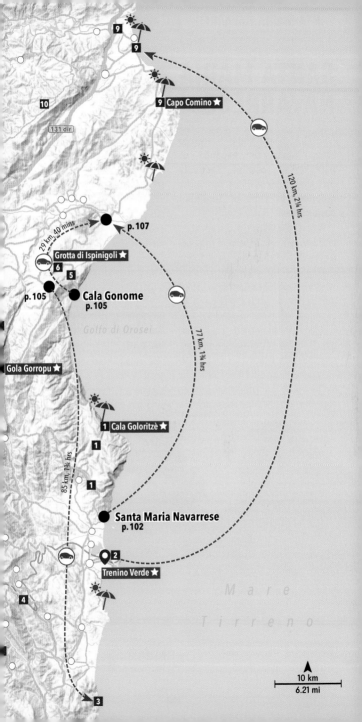

9 Capo Comino ★

9

10

131 dir

29 km, 40 mins

6
5

Grotta di Ispinigoli ★

p. 107

p. 105

Cala Gonome
p. 105

Golfo di Orosei

120 km, 2¼ hrs

77 km, 1¾ hrs

Gola Gorropu ★

85 km, 1¾ hrs

1 Cala Goloritzè ★

1

1

Santa Maria Navarrese
p. 102

2

Trenino Verde ★

4

3

Mare

Tirreno

10 km
6.21 mi

SANTA MARIA NAVARRESE

(🗺 G9) **At Santa Maria Navarrese (pop. 1,500) an expanse of pancake-flat coastline suddenly hits the stony wall of the rocky, mountainous cliffs of Sardinia's eastern coast.**

All over the village, at the entrance to the church and in front of its popular resorts and charming small hotels, 1,000-year-old olive trees cling to their territory, established here long before the Sardinians settled this patch of coastline. A fine example, which also provides much-needed shade for guests, is the *L'Olivastro* bar on a terrace above the beach.

Enjoy a drink (and live music) on the terrace at *Toma (tomaristorante.it)*, high above the harbour and watch the boats go in and out of the walled port, while planning which one to take up the coast the next day. You can book small charters from companies like *Fuorirotta (Via Lungomare 47 | tel. 32 71 97 13 94 | fuorirottacharter.it)* or take one of the larger boats run by *Nuovo Consorzio Maritimo (tel. 07 82 62 80 24 | mareogliastra.com)*, which drop off and pick up from various points along the coast. Lots of the good beaches in the area are best reached by boat: *(Cala Goloritzè, Codula di Sisine Cala Mariolu, Cala dei Gabbiani and Cala Biriola among others)*.

EATING & DRINKING

NASCAR

This small hotel restaurant serves great seafood in a charming setting, especially for those seated on its stunning terrace. *Closed for lunch | Viale*

Even the wild pigs seem to enjoy the view at Sa Pedra Longa

Pedras 1 | tel. 07 82 61 53 14 | nascar-hotel.eu | €€€

AROUND SANTA MARIA NAVARRESE

⬛ BAUNEI, SU GOLGO & CALA GOLORITZÈ

9km northwest of Santa Maria /
15 mins on the SS 125

The road to Baunei works its way up and round the mountains via a series of hairpin bends. One detour you absolutely have to take on the way is to the 80-m-high jagged rocky needle at *Sa Pedra Longa*. Steep staircases take you down to the water's edge where the rocks do not form a beach in the traditional sense but do make for some of the best snorkelling on the island. Once you see the view, you won't even resent paying the slightly cheeky supplement to sit on the terrace at *Trattoria Pedra Longa (May–Oct daily | tel. 34 71 26 98 18 | €€).*

The mountainous village of *Baunei* is a ribbon development along the main road that sits on top of a mountain ledge, high above the plain below and hemmed in by dramatic rocky outcrops and a few peaks. There are amazing views from the bars along the main road.

To reach the plateau at *Su Golgo*, it is a further 12km from Baunei along windy, and in places very steep, mountain roads (which you will share with

the local sheep). The road comes to an end at the small pilgrims' chapel of *San Pietro*, from where a well-signed path takes you to *Su Sterru*, an enormous, 270-m rocky gorge. You will find delicious, simple shepherd's cooking at *Locanda Il Rifugio – Golgo (daily | tel. 36 87 02 89 80 | coopgoloritze.com | €),* which also acts as the central point for the network of footpaths, bridleways and mountain-bike routes in the area. You can also book guided tours and climbing trips here.

On a mountain bike, it is then 13km following a mountain stream the whole way to the stunning cove of *Codula di Sisine.* ★ 🏖 *Cala Goloritzè* is said to be one of the most beautiful beaches in the world, and part of its charm lies in the fact it is so hard to reach and boats are forbidden to moor here. From the well-signed and supervised car park at *Su Sinniperu*, it is a 90-minute walk down to the small bay, which sits under a 100-m needle of rock and whose entrance on one side is marked by a stunning natural arch. Get there early as access to the cove is limited to a set number of visitors, and in the afternoon the entire bay sits in the shade of the mountains behind it. 🚏 *G9*

⬛ ARBATAX

13km south of Santa Maria / 20 mins on the SS 125

This small port town (pop. 1,500) sits on a peninsula whose red porphyry cliffs are one of Sardinia's natural wonders. They are set back from the entrance to the port where a ferry from

Cagliari to Civitavecchia stops once a week to link this forgotten region to the wider world.

Partly thanks to the ferry port, Arbatax is better known than the capital of Ogliastra, the much larger but no less sleepy town of *Tortoli* (pop. 11,000), which is 5km further inland. Tortoli's fishermen's cooperative *Ittiturismo La Peschiera (in the season daily | tel. 07 82 66 44 15 | pescatortoli.it)* serves a set menu for a very reasonable 37 euros per head every evening in their beautiful garden just at the point where the laguna meets the sea. It includes a dessert and drinks and, more importantly, enormous quantities of fish caught by the co-op's members.

The best swimming spots here (as popular with the locals as tourists) are the small cove of *Porto Frailis* or the beach of *Spiaggia di Basaùra* a mile or so down the coast. A bit further away,

Lido di Orrì is a special place with its flat expanse of sand occasionally interrupted by rocks and small cliffs rounded by the sea into dome-like formations. The prettiest beach in the area is, however, ⚓ *Spiaggia Cea*, a sandy inlet with crystal-clear water. The sea here is as calm as a swimming pool thanks to the photogenic porphyry needles which stick out of the azure sea at the bay's entrance. 📖 *G9*

3 MARINA DI GAIRO

32km south of Santa Maria / 45 mins on the SS 125, take the exit after Bari Sardo

You may have to force your jaw back into its usual position after you have first taken in the view of the rocky landscape around Marina di Gairo. Just past the picture-postcard cove of *Su Sirboni* – whose white sands appear to reflect the sun's light even brighter thanks to the red cliffs around them

A stunning setting and an unmissable art gallery: Ulassai

– an old sign reading "al mare" will show you the way to Sardinia's largest pebbly beach, the *Spiaggia Coccorrocci*. A little way inland, nature has carved out an almost perfect swimming pool at the 👯 *Piscine Naturali*. With a series of small pools and mini waterfalls linked by a network of channels, the landscape here forms a fantastic natural water park. 🗺 *G10*

INSIDER TIP
Natural waterslides

4 LANUSEI & ULASSAI

25km southwest from Santa Maria to Lanusei / 35 mins on the SS 125 and SS 198

Lanusei, with its amazing views down to the sea is the old capital of Ogliastra and its steep streets and tall buildings mean it still has a distinctly urban air. If you are peckish, quel your hunger with a portion of *culurgiones* in *Ristorante Pizzeria Ka.Mi.Ste Hotel Belvedere (closed Wed evenings | Via Umberto I 24 | tel. 0 78 24 29 84 | €)*.

A good half an hour's drive further towards the southwest, the village of *Ulassai* clings precariously to a steep mountain slope in the shade of huge, jagged rocks – it does not get much more spectacular. The old station building has been converted into one of Sardinia's best contemporary art galleries: the *Stazione dell'Arte (daily tours 9.30am, 11am, 1pm, 2.30pm, 6pm; May–Sept also 7.30pm; Oct–April also 4pm | ⏱ 1 hr)*. Containing one of the best collections of Maria Lai's work – one of Sardinia's greatest artistic talents – the gallery has over 150 of her pictures, sculptures and installations.

A narrow road out of Ulassai takes you up the slope to 👯 *Grotta Su Marmuri (tours April daily 11am, 2.30pm, 5pm; May–July and Sept 11am, 2pm, 4pm, 6pm; Aug 11am, 1pm, 3pm, 5pm, 6.30pm; Oct 11am and 2.30pm | grottasumarmuri.it | ⏱ 2 hrs)*. The cave is closed in winter in order to allow the resident bat colonies to hibernate in peace. However, this should not put you off a winter visit to Ulassai as a good outdoor alternative can be found just 6km outside the village at the *Lequarci cliffs*. From January to May, this landscape transforms into a huge waterfall as the mountain streams swell and find the shortest routes to the sea. 🗺 *F9–10*

INSIDER TIP
Wonderful winter waterfall

TRENINO VERDE ★ ☂

"The Little Green Train" is a narrow-gauge railway which snakes its way through the wild, romantic mountains. Timetables and routes are changed regularly but the stretch from Arbatax to Gairo nearly always operates. *treninoverde.com | 🗺 E-G 9–10*

DORGALI & CALA GONONE

(🗺 *G8*) **A large farming and shepherd village, *Dorgali* (pop. 8,600) is well tucked in behind the** mountains and, as a result, was invisible to pirates out at sea.

Its secret has not stayed hidden, and today it is a mecca for people who want a holiday with some active elements. However, it is not far from the beach – a small tunnel connects it to *Cala Gonone*, a charming and very green resort. To get down to the sea, you have to take the "panorama road", each of whose switchbacks offers a new stunning view of the Med!

SIGHTSEEING

ACQUARIO DI CALA GONONE 🐾

Tickle a stingray and look a dogfish in the eye. This aquarium and its 24 tanks offer an up-close and personal view into an underwater world. *Via La Favorita | opening times vary, see website for details | acquariocalagonone.it | ◷ 1½ hrs*

EATING & DRINKING

AGRITURISMO DIDONE

In a remote spot on the road towards Orosei, this organic *agriturismo* farm has wonderful views down to the coast and is just a few minutes' drive from lots of beautiful beaches. *Dinner only | SS 125 km 212.8 | tel. 34 03 79 19 36 | agriturismodidone.com | €€*

WIKIPIZZA 🍕

A pizzeria in Dorgali's centre where you can order unusual types of pizza – all the ingredients come from the island. *Daily | Via La Marmora 87 | tel. 34 90 74 24 13 | wikipizzadavittorio.it | €*

BEACHES

Cala Gonone's beach is partly artificial, but it is very clean and ideal for a cooling dip after a long walk. *Cala Fuili* is the only beach on the *Gulf of Orosei* accessible by car. From here you can walk down to *Cala Luna,* which is home to spectacular coastal caves (there is also a shuttle ferry service).

AROUND DORGALI & CALA GONONE

5 PARCO MUSEO S'ABBA FRISCA 🐾

6km north of Cala Gonone / 15 mins on Via Codula e' Gostui

An excellent place for families to spend a day out, this large park landscaped with waterfalls, ponds and small streams is home to a romantic old mill and a blacksmith as well as a tortoise enclosure. *April/May and Oct daily guided tours 11am, 12pm, 3pm, 4pm; June and Sept 10am–6pm; July/ Aug 9am–7pm | sabbafrisca.com | ◷ 1½ hr | 🏠 G8*

6 GROTTA DI ISPINIGOLI ★ ☂

11km north of Cala Gonone / 25 mins via Parco Museo S'Abba Frisca

Entering a cave from above is a pretty special experience, especially at the height of a Sardinian summer. As you come in, you pass one of Europe's tallest stalagmites at 38m. After that, you enter a magical network of caves with stalagmites and stalagtites coming at you from almost every angle. Archaeological evidence suggests that the Phoenicians were aware of these caves and some speculate they may even have sacrificed virgins in them. *Tours on the hour, April/May and Oct daily 10am-12pm and 3-5pm; June and Sept 10am-5pm; July 10am-6pm; Aug 10am-7pm | ⏱ 1 hr | ⊞ G8*

7 GOLA GORROPU ★
15km south of Dorgali / 30 mins on the SS 125

Gorropu (also called Su Goroppu or Su Gorruppu) is one of Europe's deepest gorges with its cliffs rising to heights above 400m. According to ancient legend (still recounted by an older generation of Sardinians), this was once home to the devil. Others say that trolls used to play marbles with the boulders in the deepest part of the canyon. There are several ways to get

here including a 90-minute walk along the occasionally very steep Genna-Silana Pass, just off the SS 125. Alternatively, park at S'Abba Arva and take a more sedate two-hour walk along the riverbed. You can also book a jeep tour. *gorropu.info | ⊞ F8*

8 TISCALI
15km south west of Dorgali / 30 mins on the SS 125

Hide and seek in the prehistoric age would have been pretty cool! This collapsed megalithic complex would have offered plenty of space to spread out while the seeker counted. More seriously, the network of underground chambers here would have made the local nuraghic people more or less invisible to invading attackers; and the 70 or so huts they had here would have also provided cool protection against the summer heat.

A paved road takes you from Dorgali to the Ponte Barva bridge. From here, it is a two-hour walk on a

Cala Fuili can only be reached by boat

stony and occasionally slippery path to the prehistoric cave village. Once there, you will have to pay 5 euros to get in. *Daily 9am-5pm, May-Oct 9am-7pm | ☐ F8*

OROSEI

(☐ G7) **There are worse places to spend a bit of time than Orosei (pop. 6,900). This small town at the mouth of the Cedrino river is set among orchards and vegetable farms and has a lot to offer fans of culture and nature alike.**

Tall churches rise from the network of narrow streets and dominate the town's skyscape – one advantage of this is that navigation here is easy. As a result, the best way to explore the town is to aimlessly wander as you take in old palaces, churches, the ruins of the medieval castle and the Pisan water tower.

EATING & DRINKING

BELOHORIZONTE
Wonderful seafood and an impressive view over the town. *Daily | Via Giuseppe Dessì 25 | tel. 07 84 99 11 22 | €€*

SPORT & ACTIVITIES

BOAT TRIPS
Orosei may well have given the gulf here its name but you still need a boat to get to any of its beaches. *Crociere Cala Gonone (calagononecrociere.it)* offers day trips from Orosei, La Caletta and Cala Gonone.

BEACHES

Between the mouth of the Cedrino river and Osalla Bay, there is a long expanse of beach bordered by maritime pine trees. The parasols of the largest resort on the island occupy much of the beach's central section, but you won't have any problems finding a quiet corner a little bit further down the beach. North of the river's mouth there is a series of coves and bays around *Cala Ginepro* and *Cala Liberotto* – the latter being one of the most popular beaches on the east coast. There are a couple of larger hotels and a few villas here to show that you aren't the first tourists to have discovered this spot.

A bit further north, you will find the breathtakingly beautiful nature reserve of *Oasi di Biderosa (May-Oct daily 7.30am-8pm | tel. 34 23 55 99 75 | oasibiderosa.it)*. There are five small coves here where you can swim. If you want to come by car, make sure to book a parking space in advance. There are only 140 spaces for cars and 30 for motorbikes *(costing 12 and 6 euros respectively)*. Pedestrians and cyclists are not subject to any entry limits so it may well be worth giving yourself a bit of a workout!

INSIDER TIP
Get active on the way to paradise

The beach at *Berchida* (access road off the SS 125 between Capo Comini and Sos Alinos) is very long and seems very far from the island's touristy resorts, especially whenever the white cows from a nearby farm come down to the beach to sunbathe. From there, it is about 20 minutes' walk south to the beaches around Biderosa.

AROUND OROSEI

🟑 CAPO COMINO, LA CALETTA & POSADA

34km north from Orosei La Caletta / 40 mins on the coastal road

★ ⛱ *Capo Comino* is pretty close to perfection. Pine trees, dunes and soft white sand which stretches all the way to S'Ena e Sa Chitta. You can walk for miles along the beach or take a shady stroll through the trees. Massive Saracen towers keep watch over two villages, *Santa Lucia* and ⛱ *La Caletta*, which have developed into popular mini resorts. If you wake up and open the front door in a holiday cottage here, you can almost jump on to the beach. La Caletta and Santa Lucia are also excellent places to stay for those interested in water sports. Surfers and sailors of all varieties will find plenty of options here.

The charming medieval village of *Posada* sits proudly on the top of the cliffs around the bay. In its middle, the tower of the *Castello della Fava (daily 9am-1pm and 3-6pm, in summer open all day until 1hr before sunset)* juts up towards the heavens. It is well worth climbing to the top (even for those scared of heights) to see the literally breathtaking views. 🕮 *G6-7*

🔟 MONTE ALBO

50km to Guzzurra/1 hr via Lula

This prominent white mountain ridge just south of Siniscola is difficult to miss. Motorbike riders love the traffic-free winding roads on the northwestern side of the chalk cliffs, but only very few walkers ever make the trip. To do so, park at the old forestry base at Cantoniera Guzzurra and then walk for about an hour up to the remote plateau of *Punta Su Mutucrone*. When you get back down, a plate of antipasti and local wine will not just be well earned but virtually compulsory at *Locanda Ammentos: closed in the evenings and between Oct and Easter | tel. 34 96 72 38 63 | € | 🕮 F-G7*

INSIDER TIP
Adventure then antipasti

A warm welcome awaits you in Orosei

THE INTERIOR

MOUNTAINS, SHEEP & WATERPUMPS

At around 1,800m, Sardinia's highest peaks, the Gennargentu mountains, are not especially high. That said, in contrast to the rolling hills of the Barbagia region, the craggy crenellations of the Supramonte in the northeast, and the flat volcanic plateaux in the south, they could easily be confused with the Himalaya.

The Romans rudely named Barbagia, "the land of the Barbarians", after they were unable to conquer its mountains and valleys. The name has stuck partly because the *Barbaricini* – as the population of

The inaccessible Gennargentu mountains remain the land of the shepherd

this part of the island call themselves – never fell to any subsequent invaders and maintained their own mountainous culture.

Legal codes? Who cares! Every village here worked out its own way to govern. Those that did not agree with the system in one place could just pack their bags and move on to the next. To this day, the rejection of state power (and its institutions) forms an important part of the *murales* painted on the walls of many Barbagia homes.

THE INTERIOR

Illorai

Bolòtana/Bolotana

Sindia/Sindia

Bortigali/Bortigale

Lei

Silanos/Silanus

Macumere/Macomèr

Bìroro/Birori

Otzana/Ottana

Duarche/Dualchi

Noragugume

Aidumajore/Aidomaggiore

Sèdilo/Sedilo

131 dir

Abbasanta

Zuri

Bidoniu/Bidoni

Ilartzi/Ghilarza

Tadasune/Tadasuni

Vittoria

Ardaule/Ardauli

Neunele/Neoneli

Ula/Ulà Tirso

Busache/Busachi

Ortueri

Fordongìanus

Àllai/Allai

Samugheo

Ma

iapìccia

Arruinas/Ruinas

A Oristano

Santa Justa/Santa Giusta

Tiria

Mogoredda/Mogorella

Asuni

Làconi/Lacon

Senis

Nureci

Crastu

Sant'Anna

Useddus/Usellus

Assolu/Assolo

Geno

Pau

Escovedu

Nuragus

Abas/Ales

Sini

12 Giara di Gesturi ★

Mragaxori/Morgongiori

Crucuris/Curcuris

Gesturi

Tanca Marchese

Pompu

Simaba/Simala

Tuili

Terràba/Terralba

Siris

Su Nuraxi ★

Barumin
p.122

Uras

Mòguru/Mogoro

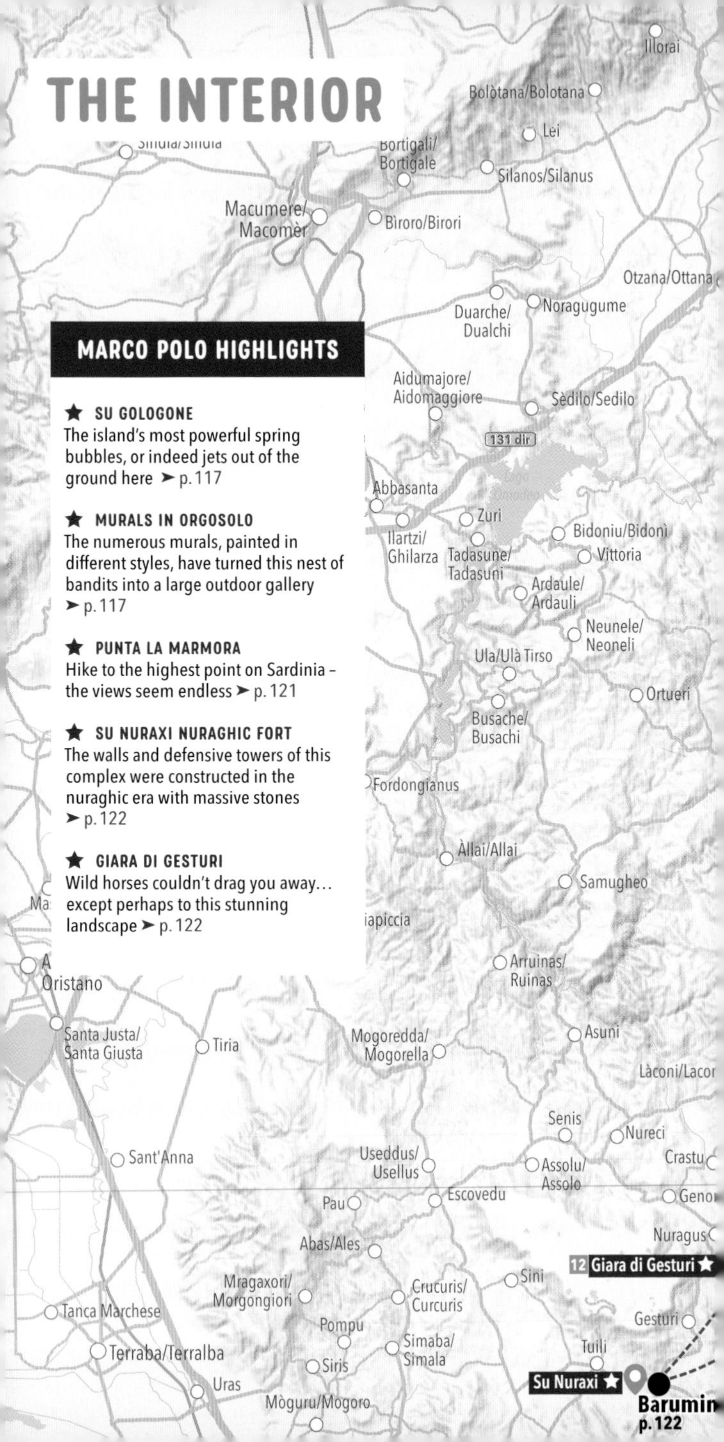

Nuoro
p. 114

1 Monte Ortobene

Su Gologone ★
3

2 Oliena

7 Orani

Sarule

5 Mamoiada

Murals in Orgosolo ★

4 Orgosolo

6 Gavoi

Lodine

6 Fonni

70 km, 90 mins

100 km, 120 mins

Oroteddi/
Orotelli

Onieri/
Oniferi

131 dir

Orzai/
Olzai

Ollollai/Ollolai

Teti

ùstis

Ovodda

Tiana/Tiana

Orthullè/
Urzulei

Talana

Sorgono

10 Tonara

8 Desulo

Brebi/Belvì

Aritzo
p. 119

Gadoni

120 km, 2½ hrs

11 Punta La Marmora ★

Biddamanna Istrisaili/
Villagrande Strisaili

Villanova Strisaili

Àrthana/
Arzana

Elini

Lanusèi/Lanusei

Seulu/
Seulo

Seui

Taquisara

Gàiru/
Gairo Sant'Elena

Òsini/Osini

53 km, 60 mins

9 Sadali

Ussassa/
Ussassai

Ulassa/
Ulassai

Jersu/
Jerzu

Istersili/Esterzili

Isili/Isili

Biddanoa 'e Tulu/
Villanova Tulo

Santuario Nuragico
di Santa Vittoria

Nurri

Serri

Arrolli/Orroli

5 km
3.11 mi

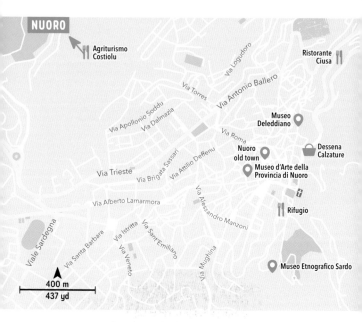

NUORO

(□ F8) **Nuoro (pop. 37,000) may not look like the prettiest of places from the outside but don't be put off by the fake marble of the Mussolini era or the modern concrete carbuncles which adorn the town's edges.**

The charming, almost village-like old town can take some finding, but it is worth it. At the beginning of the 20th century, Nuoro was little more than a tiny market town where farmers, shepherds and labourers lived in their own separate districts. The smell of sheep dung only disappeared from the city after 1927 when it became the province's capital. Nowadays it has all the amenities and institutions – from prison to bishop's palace – of a regionally important place, and its size has grown to match. Today it is the biggest town in Barbagia and, for many young Barbaricini, the modern shopping centres in the industrial Prato Sardo area act as a window onto the world beyond.

SIGHTSEEING

OLD TOWN

The grand, granite paving of *Corso Garibaldi* will take you into the middle of the old town. At the end of the street, just as you reach the tree-lined Piazza Vittorio Emanuele, take a left into a small alleyway which leads to the peaceful *Piazza Sebastiano Satta*. It is named after Barbagia's most renowned poet, who was born in

Nuoro. The square itself, with its huge granite columns, was designed by Constantino Nivola. Head on from here and across the Piazza San Giovanni to reach the Via Tola, which will take you to the doors of the neoclassical *Santa Maria della Neve* cathedral.

MUSEO D'ARTE DELLA PROVINCIA DI NUORO 🌂

This little provincial museum punches above its weight with constantly changing and extremely well-curated temporary exhibitions. These tend to focus on the best-known, modern Sardinian artists, like Giuseppe Biasi, Maria Lai, Francesco Ciusa, Mario Delitala and Constantino Nivola. *Via Sebastiano Satta 27 | Tue–Sun 10am–7pm | museoman.it | ⊙ 1 hr*

MUSEO DELEDDIANO 🌂

Grazia Deledda was the first female Italian recipient of the Nobel Prize for Literature in 1926. Although her work primarily focused on the hardships of life for poor Sardinians around 1900, the house she was born in bears witness to the fact that she herself came from a wealthy family. *Via Grazia Deledda 42 | Tue–Sun 10am–1pm and 3–7pm, mid-March–Sept until 8pm | isresardegna.it | ⊙ 30 mins*

MUSEO ETNOGRAFICO SARDO 🌂

One of the best museums on the whole island. Although the information placards are only in Italian in this ethnographic museum, the objects, images and reconstructions give a very good sense of life across many centuries of Sardinian history. *Via Mereu 56 | Tue–Sun 10am–1pm and 3–7pm, mid-March–Sept until 8pm | isresardegna.it | ⊙ 2 hrs*

EATING & DRINKING

AGRITURISMO COSTIOLU 🚩🐄

Barbagia at its best. This farmstead sits in splendid seclusion on around 100 hectares of land 10km out of town on the road towards Bitti. If you want to get an authentic taste of Barbagia, you won't do any better than here (they also run cookery courses). Almost everything you eat will have been produced on their land, and you can buy much of their produce to take home with you. They also have a small campsite with space for tents and vans. *Daily, reservation required in the evening | SS 389 km90 | tel. 07 84 26 00 88 | agriturismocostiolu.com | €*

Piazza Sebastiano Satta, Nuoro

RIFUGIO
Excellent regional food (and pizza) at reasonable prices; this trattoria in the old town is as popular among locals as visitors. *Closed Wed | Via Mereu 28/36 | tel. 07 84 23 23 55 | trattoriarifugio. com | €-€€*

RISTORANTE CIUSA
A superb wine selection and excellent food make this one of the best restaurants in town. Make sure you save some space though – the desserts are pure poetry. *Daily | Viale Francesco Ciusa 55 | tel. 07 84 25 70 52 | ristoranteciusa.it | €€-€€€*

SHOPPING

DESSENA CALZATURE
Nuoro has always been famous for leather-making, and the Dessena family has been making boots, saddles and bags (and more) to measure since the 1930s. If you buy yourself a pair of boots or a shepherd's rucksack here, it is likely your children or grandchildren will still be getting use out of it in decades to come. *Via Aspromonte 27 | dessenacalzature.todosmart.net*

AROUND NUORO

1 MONTE ORTOBENE
6km east of Nuoro / a good 10 mins on the SS 129 and the SP 42
A winding road takes you up to the 955-m peak of Nuoro's nearest mountain. Its granite rock formations and many trees offer shady spots for picnics. At its top, there is a bronze statue of the Redeemer – it is said that stroking his big toe will bring you good luck. You may think you are already seeing the results once you get a look at the view down to the city and to the Supramonte and Gennargentu mountains beyond. *□ F8*

2 OLIENA
10km southeast of Nuoro / 15 mins on the SP 22
This charming village (pop. 7,200) is best known for Nepente (a Cannonau red wine), its richly embroidered local dress and its culinary delicacies. Thanks to its position at the foot of *Monte Corrasi* (1,463m), it has become something of a regional centre for outdoor activities. Despite the fact there is plenty of infrastructure for tourists here, it has retained much of its own atmosphere. On the slopes of Monte Maccione, high above the village a cooperative called *Enis* serves traditional food with especially good cheese and *salsiccia* antipasti under the

INSIDER TIP
Wild walks and wonderful wine

shade of a grove of oak trees. *(Closed for lunch | tel. 07 84 28 83 63 | coope nis.it | €-€€.)* After a hearty evening meal here, you will, however, not have much time to complete a five-hour walk in the Monte Corrasi range (aka "Sardinia's Dolomites"). Instead, ask for a room and take advantage of the restaurant's breathtaking roof

One of Orgosolo's famous murals

terrace's views over Nuoro. Then you can work off your meal the next day. *III F8*

3 SU GOLOGONE

18km south east of Nuoro / 25 mins on the SP 22 and SP 46

Sardinia's most powerful spring brings more than 500 litres of water to the surface every second. A splash of blue among chalky rocks, the water appears to burst out of a mountain crevice. There are taps dispensing cool drinking water and a small café offering drinks and snacks. All in all, it is an idyllic place to relax. The hotel of the same name is furnished with Sardinian antiques and modern crafted objects. Its restaurant serves excellent, beautifully presented Barbagia cuisine. *Closed for lunch| tel.*

07 84 28 75 12 | sugologone.it | €€€ | III F8

4 ORGOSOLO 🐗

20km south of Nuoro / 30 mins on the SP 58

Probably Sardinia's most famous village (pop. 4,300), it even features on large bus tour itineraries. This village of vendettas, bandits and rebellion against the state appears fairly normal at first glance, just with a slightly higher than average number of unfinished buildings. What is unusual, however, are the large police barracks and the many ★ *murales*. The murals are a clear expression of the social concerns of the locals: unemployment and emigration, the social situation of the shepherds, discrimination against the Sardinians in their own country, and the arrogance of politicians. An idea picked up from Latin America, the murals are painted on house walls as a protest against poverty and repression, police, bureaucracy and the military. They have become well known all over the world.

A narrow road leads across the wild, romantic plateau of Pratobello into the *Foresta di Montes,* one of the most beautiful and pristine areas of Barbagia. The road ends at a forestry station with an information point. From here there is an uphill walk through the forest to the *Funtana Bona* spring with picnic facilities, and further on to the striking rock needle of *Monte Novo San Giovanni* (1,316m).⠀*F8*

5 MAMOIADA

20km south of Nuoro / 20 mins on the fast road SS 389var

This remote rural village owes its fame to its dark carnival in which, since time immemorial, the *mamuthones* (creatures hiding behind scarily distorted black masks, and hung with heavy bells and draped in furs) and *issohadores* (wearing colourful costumes and grinning white masks) have taken to the streets. Find out more about this ancient ritual in the small yet very interesting *Museo delle Maschere (Piazza Europa 15 | Tue-Sun 9am-1pm and 3-7pm | museodellemaschere.it).*

One of the last mask carvers on the island is *Ruggero Mameli (Via Crisponi 19 | mascheremameli.com),* whose workshop you can visit. Those wanting to take a closer look at the masks can do so at his *mask exhibition (Corso*

Vittorio Emanuele III), where he has assembled over 200 of these impressive works of art. This exhibition is open to the public.

All this talk of masks making you thirsty? Then don't miss buying one of the award-winning wines from the *Cantina Giuseppe Sedilesu (Via Vittorio Emanuele II 64 | giuseppesedilesu.com).* A bottle of Mamuthone or Cannonau wine is sure to make you very popular back home. ⠀*F8*

6 FONNI & GAVOI

33km to Fonni south of Nuoro / 30 mins on the fast road SS 389var

Fonni is the island's highest village. New buildings mingle with old stone houses. The village is a good base for excursions into the Gennargentu massif. On the mountain road towards Desulo a side road branches off towards *Monte Spada* (1,595m), which ends at the valley's ski-lift station. The ski lift is in need of restoration but there is not enough money for it yet, so the only way to *Punta La Marmora* in on foot (return trip approx. five hours).

The neighbouring village of *Gavoi* has a pretty, historic centre and is surrounded by forests and mountain pastures with tall oaks. In the village, the *Santa Rughe* restaurant *(daily | tel. 0 78 45 37 74 | €-€€)* serves delicious traditional, local fare and also pizzas. ⠀*E8-9*

7 ORANI

20km southwest of Nuoro / 25 mins on SS 389 until you see signs

It is little known that Constantino

Mamuthones roam the streets of Mamoiada during carnival

Nivola, the world-famous painter and sculptor, was born in this small, unprepossessing village. The old washhouse in the village has been converted into the *Museo Nivola (Thu–Tue 10.30am–1.30pm and 3.30–7.30pm, Fri/Sat until 8pm | Via Gonare 2 | museonivola.it)* in his honour. Its beautifully landscaped, modernised buildings and gardens have been converted into a small contemporary art gallery which can compete with the best in the world. The Magna-Mater marble sculptures are particularly striking – on a closer look, they resemble bright white angels. Orani also offers you an opportunity to buy tailor-made corduroy – the father and son team at Modolo have been working hard to keep up with the renewed fashion interest in this traditional fabric. *Sartoria Modolo (Corso Garibaldi 141 | sartoriamodolo.com)* | *E8*

ARITZO

(*E9*) **The western slopes of the Gennargentu are a green oasis filled with dense chestnut woods and cork tree plantations.**

The village of Aritzo (pop. 1,300) – which sits at 800m above sea level – has the highest density of springs in Sardinia. Umberto I, King of Italy, was a fan of this spot for its beautiful views and pleasant mountain air. Today, most of its fame comes from chestnuts and from *Monte Texile*, a particularly striking rock formation considered sacred by the nuraghic people.

EATING & DRINKING

DA DADDO

Wait for the food before you judge this place. It does not look much from outside, but its excellent pizza and local mushroom (or occasionally wild boar) specials will have you coming back again and again. *Closed Mon | Viale Kennedy 14 | tel. 38 89 28 96 49 | €*

SA MUVARA

One of the most famous restaurants in Aritzo is in the four-star hotel of the same time. Its excellent mountain food is only matched by the beautiful surroundings of the hotel's extensive gardens (on the southern edge of the village). *May–Nov daily | Viale Kennedy 33 | tel. 07 84 62 93 36 | www.samuvarahotel.com/it | €€€*

Sadali waterfall

AROUND ARITZO

🟦 DESULO

17km northeast of Aritzo / 30 mins by car on the SS 295 and the SP 7

Like many of the villages in Barbagia, Desulo is a centre for Sardinian culture and traditions. If you think that nobody would swap fast fashion for traditional dress anymore, you will get a bit of a shock here as women wander around in their bright red dresses. The village is also known for its hearty salami. *⊞ E9*

🟦 SADALI

35km south of Aritzo / 50 mins by car on the SP 8

This small village lies on the edge of a broad, sweeping plateau. The older houses here are built into the mountain where it begins to slope down, while the more modern ones are on the flat summit. Narrow lanes take you down to the villagers' gardens and the water mill in the valley. Small streams babble out of every nook and cranny, and right in the middle of the village there is an extremely romantic (reflected in its name) waterfall – the *Cascata di San Valentino.*

However, it does not stop there. The 🐵 *Su Stampu de su Turrunu* is a unique geological phenomenon. A small pool in a cave under a waterfall – half the day it fills up with water and then it begins spewing water down the mountain. To get there, park at the *Is*

INSIDER TIP
In need of shower?

Janas (May–Sept daily 10am–1pm and 3–6pm) cave. If the walk down and back has awoken your hunger, there is excellent mountain food to be had in *Ristorante Alle Grotte (same opening hours as the cave | tel. 34 83 95 88 77 | €–€€)*, which is near the cave entry and set in a beautiful wild landscape. *E–F10*

🔟 TONARA & SORGONO

25km northwest from Aritzo to Sorgono / 45 mins by car via Tonara

The road starts off following the railway tracks before it begins an ascent through the forests up to *Tonara*. This small village is known around Sardinia for *torrone*, a sweet treat made from egg whites, honey and nuts, and for the livestock bells which are produced here and heard all across the island. There are also active woodworking and weaving workshops here, as well as a brilliant exhibition of wooden and granite sculptures by Sardinian artists such as Antonio Sini, Tonino Loi and Pinuccio Sciola on the main road. The *Locanda Su Muggianeddu (closed Fri | tel. 0 78 46 38 85 | €)* serves authentic, home-made mountain grub. Make sure you try the lamb stew – *agnello in umido.*

Sorgono, the neighbouring village, is famous for Mandrolisai – a delicious red wine which is only produced in Sorgono. Wine buffs should pay a visit to *Cantina del Mandrolisai (Corso IV Novembre 20 | cantinadelmandrolisai.com)* who name their wines after the many villagers who have lived to be over 100 here. Is the wine responsible for this large number of centenarions? *E9*

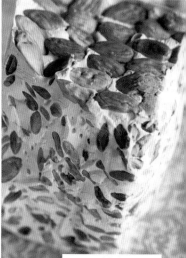

Dentists' delight: Torrone

🔟🔟 PUNTA LA MARMORA ⭐

22km east of Aritzo / 50 mins to the car park

At Tascusi, where the roads from Fonni, Desulo and Tonara meet, take the road towards S'Arena. This will take you up to the restricted area at 1,510m. From here, you have to follow the Arcu Artilai ridge to get to the highest point on the island. Hiking up on the "roof of Sardinia " means that, on a clear day, you get stunning views over both the east and west coasts. If you set off in the evening, you can watch the sun going down in the west and pitch a tent at the mountain hut *Rudere Rifugio La Marmora,* which has a water source and a fence to protect from animals. The next morning you can watch the sunrise over the edge of Sardinia – a once in a lifetime moment. *F9*

INSIDER TIP
Spectacular sunrise

BARUMINI

(📖 E10) **This small agricultural town had no great significance until Su Nuraxi was uncovered and it became a hotspot for tourists interested in prehistoric Sardinia.**

However, Barumini had had a previous golden age in the medieval period, which was when the grand village church and manor house, Casa Zapata, were built.

SIGHTSEEING

SU NURAXI NURAGHIC FORT ★
In 1949 after several days of heavy rain, a landslide started on a hill here. It did not last long, but in its wake a series of old walls and the footprints of old buildings were revealed for the first time in thousands of years. The nuraghic fort discovered here is so impressive that it was later declared a UNESCO World Heritage Site. It served both as a fortress and as the home of a powerful local tribe. With four towers around the outside and one in the middle, the citadel was surrounded by a thick, fortified wall, outside of which the 150 houses of the village stood. Some served as workshops, evidence of which can still be seen today. After listening to a guide introducing you to the site and looking out across the stunning Marmilla landscape, your imagination will find it very easy to picture nuraghic people running around this settlement. The entry fee also covers the museum in the *Casa Zapata*. Another nuraghe, discovered underneath the *palazzo* here, has been partially excavated. You can also walk around the late Stone Age walls on glass walkways. There is a small archaeological and anthropological exhibition in the museum. *Daily 9am–5pm, March–Oct 9am until 1 hr before sunset | fondazionebarumini.it |* 🕐 *2 hrs*

SARDEGNA IN MINIATURA 👥
It does pretty much what it says on the tin. Sardinian and global monuments in miniature, from famous sights on the island to a dinosaur park and planetarium. *Mid-March–Sept daily 9am–6pm | sardegnainminiatura.it*

EATING & DRINKING

SA LOLLA
You can feast on delicious Sardinian specialities under the arches of this restaurant. *Daily Nov–April Sat/Sun only | Via Cavour 49 | tel. 07 09 36 84 19 | €€*

AROUND BARUMINI

🔢 GIARA DI GESTURI ★ 👥 🐗
10km northwest of Barumini / 20 mins by car via Tuili
This 12-km-long and 5-km-wide basalt plateau is covered in thick scrub and cork oak trees. In winter, large bodies of water form all over the impermeable basalt. Around 600 wild horses live here alongside goats,

sheep and pigs. Wild or tame? Well, somewhere in the middle. All the animals are basically free to roam but are registered; they are provided with water from vehicles in summer when life's most vital nectar is in short supply.

⓭ SANTUARIO NURAGICO DI SANTA VITTORIA

20km east of Barumini/ 30 mins by car on the SP 5 and the SP 9

The craggy basalt plateau of *Giara di Serri* was one of the most important centres of nuraghic culture. Beginning

The wonderfully well-preserved nuraghe Su Nuraxi in Barumini

There are quite a few one-way tracks that criss-cross the plateau. The best place to start getting a sense of this unusual landscape is Tuili, which houses a delightful Baroque church. Follow the signs for "Altopiano della Giara" in the village's narrow streets. From the car park you will have to go the rest of the way on foot, or you can "borrow" a bike from Mr Asfo. He will gladly take a donation in return... *D-E10*

where today's Santa Vittoria chapel seems to float above the gently rolling hills of Marmilla behind it, the nuraghic people had one of their most important pilgrimage sites. There was a temple complex here and an oval stadium where people came to test their skills against each other. The underground sacred well here has survived amazingly well. *Daily 9am–sunset | ⏱ 2 hrs ▢ E10*

INSIDER TIP
Ancient stadium

DISCOVERY TOURS

Want to get under the skin of the region? Then our discovery tours provide the perfect guide – they include great tips on where to go and what to see, plus the best places for a bite to eat and a selection of fun activities.

① ROUND TRIP THROUGH RURAL GALLURA

- ➤ Cruise through culture on curving country roads
- ➤ Pick up some produce then have a picnic
- ➤ Take in the view all the way to Corsica

📍	Arzachena	🏁	Arzachena
↻	Approx. 150km	🚗	1 day (4 hrs total driving time)
ℹ	If you tackle this tour on a Wednesday, you can take in the weekly market at Arzachena		

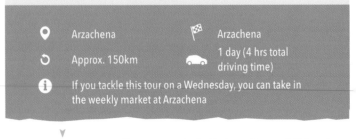

① Arzachena

The tour starts in the lively small town of ① Arzachena ➤ p. 50, whose luxury supermarkets more than satisfy

Idyllic Cala di Luna can be visited as part of a combined walking and boat tour

the needs of tourists on the Costa Smeralda with champagne and caviar. Fill your picnic basket with delicacies – with any luck you will be there on a Wednesday and can do so at the market, whose stalls spread out over *the central piazza and surrounding streets.* Before you get in the car, take a little walk to the Fungo, the vast piece of granite that has been moulded by wind and rain into the shape of a huge mushroom.

STOP FOR A PICNIC IN A RUINED CASTLE

Take the SS 427 towards Sant'Antonio di Gallura and turn right at the first crossroads onto the SP 14 towards Luogosanto. After about 4km follow the sign to "Tomba Coddu Vecchiu" and turn left. Keep going until you reach ❷ Coddu Vecchiu, *a well-preserved giant Stone Age tomb in the middle of a field. Follow the track for another 1km (making sure you keep to the left), and you'll get to the impressive nuraghic complex of* La Prisgiona. *Back on the SP 14 towards Lugosanto, after just a few bends in this wonderfully hilly landscape, you will reach a picnic spot in the shade of a huge ancient olive tree. Pull in here and enjoy your picnic before heading up the steep but very pretty path to* ❸ Castello di Balaiana *and the* charming small church of San Leonardo.

7 km   40 mins

❷ Coddu Vecchiu

13 km   1 hr

❸ Castello di Balaiana

5 km   15 mins

About 1km before Luogosanto, turn left and follow the narrow tarmac road up the mountain for about 1km to the enchanting church of ④ *San Trano. In the tiny mountain village of* ⑤ Luogosanto ➤ p. 51 *("Holy place") stop for a coffee at the inviting* Bar Museo *(daily | Via Carducci) on the Piazza Gallura. After Luogosanto, follow the bends of the SP 14 downhill, and soon you'll get to the SS 133. Turn left towards* ⑥ Tempio Pausania ➤ p. 46. *Enjoy a stroll through the pleasant granite town, then head out on the SS 392 towards Oschiri. After 8km, a two-lane road turns left in the wood and takes you along endless bends up Monte Limbara.*

THE MOST RELAXED WAY
TO CLIMB A MOUNTAIN

After 6km of twisting, turning roads up the mountain through the loveliest mountain landscape, you'll reach the settlement of ❼ Vallicciola, 1000m above sea level. You'll find delightful picnic places with cool spring water for a picnic at altitude in the refreshing mountain air. The road becomes narrower and poorer after Vallicciola, ending at the statue of the Madonna della Neve, from where you have panoramic views of the whole of northern Sardinia and it's only about a 15-minute walk up to the top of Monte Limbara.

INSIDER TIPP
Pedestrian peak

HAVE YOU EVER SEEN SO MANY MAJESTIC
OLIVE TREES?

Then head back down to Tempio, and continue along the SS 127 towards Calangianus. Just before you get to the town, turn left towards Luras, then take the first right at the next fork, and follow the SP 136 to the Lago di Liscia reservoir. A short distance from the reservoir is a small sign pointing left to "Olivastri Millenari" on the SP 137 (dead end), which will take you along the north side of the lake to the famous ❽ Olivastri Millenari ➤ p. 46. *It's another 5km or so to the little country church of San Bartolomeo where you can park. From here, it is* a very short walk to three ancient, very healthy wild olive trees, one of which is Europe's oldest specimen and has a 25-m crown.

Return to the main road and head northeast towards Sant' Antonio di Gallura and back to ❶ Arzachena.

The famous 4,000-year-old olive tree

| 25 km | 25 mins |

❼ Vallicciola

| 39 km | 1 hr |

❽ Olivastri Millenari

| 35km | 40 mins |

❶ Arzachena

② COVERING THE COVES ON FOOT

➤ Challenging hiking and a relaxed boat trip back
➤ A 10-km walk along an unspoiled coastline
➤ A superb natural coastal arch

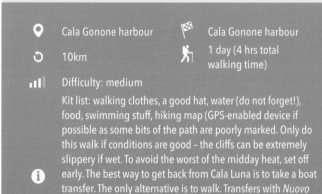

📍 Cala Gonone harbour   🏁 Cala Gonone harbour

🔄 10km   🚶 1 day (4 hrs total walking time)

📶 Difficulty: medium

Kit list: walking clothes, a good hat, water (do not forget!), food, swimming stuff, hiking map (GPS-enabled device if possible as some bits of the path are poorly marked. Only do this walk if conditions are good – the cliffs can be extremely slippery if wet. To avoid the worst of the midday heat, set off early. The best way to get back from Cala Luna is to take a boat transfer. The only alternative is to walk. Transfers with *Nuovo Consorzio Trasporti Marittimi (calagononecrociere.it)*. Make sure to check their timetable and book your ticket before you leave; the boats will not wait. At the time of writing, boats left at 3.30pm, 4.30pm and 5.30pm. On some days there is also a 6.30pm connection.

❶ Cala Gonone harbour

12 km   45 mins

❷ Cala Sisine

3300 m   1¾ hrs

From the ❶ harbour in Cala Gonone start your tour *by taking a boat* along the spectacular steep coast past the delightful bay of Cala Luna – where you will end up later – to ❷ Cala Sisine with its fine, colourful sand. *The path starts at the building on the north end of the bay, and continues upwards in steep serpentine bends.* After about 20 minutes you will get to a height that allows you to take in wonderful views down to Cala Sisine and the sea, shimmering in every possible shade of blue and turquoise.

IT'S A STEEP PATH UP
(THANKFULLY IT'S SHADY)

Continue at the same height parallel to the coast for a while. The path then brings you to a dense forest, through which it takes you along numerous serpentine bends to a height of 150m. At the end of the forest

– after about an hour – you'll come to a rocky section. It's a good idea to take a breather here, because the views down to the coast and Cala Sisine are literally going to take the rest of your breath away! *Continue along a relatively flat section to the little gorge of Girrove Longu, after which comes a second steep ascent through shady forest. After about another hour and 45 minutes you'll come to the* ➌ Cuile Sacedderano, a typical traditional Sardinian shepherd's hut which offers shade in the shape of two parasol roofs and always has a well-stocked wood stack outside it. It's the perfect place to stop for a longer rest surrounded by the beauty of nature. By this point you have already climbed a total of 530m.

REACHING THE PEAK

Be careful: you need a good sense of direction and some common sense here. Follow the path that starts to the left just behind the hut and runs along the top of the gorge. After a good two hours, the tour reaches its summit at 630m. You've done the tough bit! Now it's slightly downhill, to a wide, mostly easy forest path that you follow to the right. Then the view opens up before you: the coast and your destination, the beautiful cove of Cala Luna, and in the distance Cala Gonone where you started. Enjoy the fabulous views and then crack on!

The rest of the route is now downhill. After a good three hours' total hiking, you'll come to the spectacular natural arch ➍ S'Arcada S'Architieddu Lupiru. *The view through the opening is an absolute treat! Then continue downhill through the fragrant maquis which covers the rocky landscape until you come to a dip. It can't be all downhill really, can it? No. There's one final, short ascent to overcome, and you're at* ➎ Cala Luna.

➌ **Cuile Sacedderano**

3700 m   80 mins

➍ **S'Arcada S'Architieddu Lupiru**

2800 m   55 mins

➎ **Cala Luna**

Finish with a dip at Cala Luna – your tired feet deserve it!

This legendary cove is one of the loveliest spots in the Mediterranean: a picturesque, almost 700-m–long beach, behind which the steep rocky walls open up with impressive grottos. A little stream provides water for the flowering oleanders along its banks.

GET YOUR SWIMMERS ON!

A little bridge takes you to a cosy bar and restaurant, surrounded by oleander, which serves cools drinks and fortifying meals to tired hikers. Now, at last, you can get your swimming things out and refresh yourself in the crystal-clear water, relax on the beach and then board the boat for the return trip to ❶ Cala Gonone harbour. On the way back, you can retrace your route, patting yourself on the back the whole way!

7 km   25 mins

❶ Cala Gonone harbour

❸ THE GIRO DELL'ISOLA DI SANT'ANTIOCO: AN ISLAND CYCLING ADVENTURE

➤ A lap of Italy's fourth biggest island
➤ Get to the best beaches and most beautiful cliffs and enjoy delicious seafood
➤ Spectacular spots to contemplate the world and catch your breath

📍 Sant'Antioco   🏁 Sant'Antioco

🔄 About 55km   🚲 1 day (5 hrs total cycling time)

📶 Difficulty: medium

ℹ️ Kit list: Swimming stuff, a decent hat, water, a map (we recommend Carta turistica No. 2, Da Santa Margherita to Calasetta). The entire route is on well-paved roads and paths and there are only a few relatively gentle climbs. However, due to the distance, a decent touring or mountain bike is essential. It can get extremely hot so make sure you have enough water!
Bike hire: Euromoto *(Via Nazionale 57 | tel. 07 81 84 09 07 | euromoto.info)*

Leave ❶ Sant'Antioco ➤ p. 86 *on the Via Nazionale and then go south, turning half right on the Via della Rinascita.* The road is flat and initially takes you past the saltworks, before reaching the coast where it takes you past some lovely beaches but don't succumb to temptation yet. After 8km you will reach the small resort of ❷ Maladroxia. Now you can have a rest and get in the sea for the first time on the ride! The water is generally so beautifully calm here that a quick refreshing dip is well worth it, even if the weather is not playing ball. *After Maladroxia, the road heads slightly inland before bringing you back to the coast at the long, lovely sandy beach of* ❸ Coaquaddus. During the high season, there is a little café/bar on the road along the beach. *You will then cross slightly undulating terrain until you reach the Torre Cannai.* The short detour to this Saracen

❶ Sant'Antioco

❷ Maladroxia

4 km   15 mins

❸ Coaquaddus

6 km   25 mins

tower is a must for anyone seeking romantic beauty on the coast. *The route then winds through the little village of Peonia Rosa en route to* ④ Capo Sperone, the southern tip of the island. The rugged coastal cliffs of the cape are well worth another short romantic detour!

④ Capo Sperone

THE HIGHEST POINT ON YOUR RIDE MERITS A SECOND SWIM

9 km   1 hr

From the Capo Sperone you ride inland for a good 8km towards Nuraghe Feminedda. About halfway along the route you'll pass what is, at 76m, the highest point on this stretch. Watch out at this point: if you reach the main road, you have gone too far! Instead look out for a track on the left which takes you down to the sea about 2km before you hit the road. It will take you past the monumental tomb of Su Niu e Su Crobu – which is the best selfie spot on the ride – and on to ⑤ La Tonnara. This small, isolated holiday resort with a campsite has its own lovely beach Cala Sapone, perfect for a swim. There is also a friendly beach restaurant/bar right on the road with excellent fish and seafood at low prices. It's the ideal place to rest and watch life on the beach.

⑤ La Tonnara

1 km   5 mins

CLAMBER DOWN TO THE BAY!

A short distance from La Tonnara, on the left, there is a car park in the middle of the countryside. Be sure to stop here and climb down to the ⑥ Cala della Signora! In the bay, the wind and weather have smoothed and polished the volcanic rock into extremely beautiful shapes. If the sea is calm, this is also a great spot to snorkel; however, if there are white horses on the waves, sit back and watch them crashing into the cliffs. Those interested in beauty and romance will love the next section! *Follow the narrow road as it continues along the steep stretch of coast (be careful, it sometimes gets extremely close to the edge).* The coastline here was formed by cooling volcanic rock and it sticks out against the landscape in

⑥ Cala della Signora

The flat topography of Sant'Antioco is perfect for cycling

a strikingly beautiful manner. There are plenty of viewpoints and benches for you to sit back and enjoy the stunning views.

GET DOWN TO THE TRATTORIA – YOU HAVE EARNED IT!

After about 35km of your total ride you'll come to the Spiaggia Grande, the island's biggest and most frequently visited beach. Shortly afterwards, you'll pass the first houses in ❼ Calasetta ➤ p. 87. This town, which is set out in a perfect grid, has a lot to offer passing tourists in terms of cafés, bars and restaurants. Treat yourself to a meal at the trattoria Da Pasqualino *(closed Mon | Viale Regina Margherita 85 | tel. 0 78 18 84 73 | €€)* which serves excellent food showing off the fascinating cultural heritage of the island's inhabitants.

After this very decent meal, you'll be itching to get back on the bike to work it off. *To leave Calasetta, you have to cycle along the main road towards Sant'Antioco for a short stretch. After 1.5km take the left turn off it towards Cussorgia and the relatively remote laguna of Stagno Cirdu (Lungomare Caduti Nassiriya). From here it's just around 20 relaxed minutes along the flat coastal road back to* ❶ Sant'Antioco. Watch the sun go down in the narrow channel between Sant'Antioco and the Sardinian mainland. In the golden light, with fishing boats gently rocking on the waves, this might well be the most beautiful view of the whole day … but you will only know that if you have seen them all!

14 km   1 hr

❼ Calasetta

12 km   45 mins

❶ Sant'Antioco

GOOD TO KNOW

HOLIDAY BASICS

ARRIVAL

GETTING THERE

True petrolheads can get to Sardinia by car. The best option involves driving to Genoa and then taking the long and expensive night ferry to Olbia or Porto Torres.

If you want a greener option, you can take the train to any of the ports on mainland Italy and then the train from there. However, there is little by way of rail infrastructure on the island. The line from Golf Aranci/Olbia to Cagliari is more or less the only one (there is a short branch line to Porto Torres and Iglesias too). If taking the train/ferry, route, you need at least an hour at the port to transfer. More info at *trenitalia.com* and *seat61.com*

There are year-round direct flights from the UK to Sardinia (mostly to Cagliari, but also to Olbia and Alghero in the high season). Both budget and premium carriers fly here and it is well worth comparing prices. Cagliari's airport is connected to the city via buses and trains, while Olbia only has bus connections (although these will get you to several resorts). Alghero's bus station only gets you to Alghero and Sassari without having to change.

CLIMATE & WHEN TO GO

April/May and September/October attract a lot of motorbike riders to Sardinia's winding, beautiful roads. If you want to explore or to do a lot of outdoor activities, the slightly cooler months at the beginning and end of summer are best. You can swim (at pleasant temperatures) from mid-May to the beginning of October – there are places, especially in the south, where it stays warm enough well into November. Peak season begins at the end of June and lasts until the end of August. If you

It can be breezy at Capo Spartivento on Sardinia's southernmost tip

can avoid mid-August, you should. The island is full to bursting at this time and everything books up very fast. For another side to Sardinia, come in the winter. For a few weeks in January and February, the mountains here are snow-capped and absolutely beautiful.

CUSTOMS

EU citizens can import and export goods for personal use without paying duty. The limits are 800 cigarettes, 400 cigarillos, 200 cigars or 1kg of smoking tobacco; 10 litres of spirits over 22% vol., 90 litres of wine, 110 litres of beer per adult. Citizens of other countries, e.g. the UK, USA and Canada, can import the following without paying duty: 200 cigarettes, 100 cigarillos, 50 cigars, 250g of tobacco; 1 litre of spirits over 22% vol., 2 litres of liquors or fortified wine, 16 litres of beer; 50g of perfume or 250ml of eau de toilette.

GETTING AROUND

BUS

Sardinia has an extensive bus network. The state-run ARST *(tel: 800 86 50 42 / www.arst.sardegna.it)* serves nearly every village on the island. But there is no general schedule, nor are the services synchronised. Larger places each have a municipal bus service, and the major towns have a central bus station *(stazione autobus)*; in villages, the stop is usually in the centre. Tickets can be purchased from bars, kiosks or from tobacconists around the bus stop.

VEHICLE HIRE

The cheapest option is usually to book before you travel through a large travel operator or online. A small car starts at approx. 200 euros per week.

Make sure you keep an eye on the type of insurance you get offered/sold both when booking and picking up.

HIGHWAY CODE

Apart from the obvious of driving on the right, Italian traffic regulations are similar to those in the UK. However, there are some important things to note: at crossroads, you give way to cars from the right; outside of towns car lights must be switched on at all times; and there has to be a reflective vest for every passenger in a car; these must be worn if you break down and are standing on the side of the road. The speed limit in built-up areas is 50kmh, on main roads 90kmh, on dual carriageways 110 kmh, on motorways it is 130 kmh.

Petrol stations are usually open from 7.30am–12.30pm and from 3.30-7.30pm but are closed on Sundays. Nearly all have an automated machine where you can fill up using a credit card or cash.

There are often reports of non-Italian cards being rejected in petrol stations so don't leave it to the last minute to fill up – especially if returning your rental car.

EMERGENCIES

CONSULATES & EMBASSIES
British Consulate
Cagliari: Viale La Playa, 7, Cagliari | tel. 070 828 628

US Embassy
Via Vittorio Veneto, 121, Rome | tel. 0 06 46741

Irish Embassy
Via Giacomo Medici 1, Rome | tel 0 06 5852 381

Australian Embassy
Via Antonio Bosio, 5, Rome | tel 0 06 8527 21

HEALTH
A valid EHIC/GHIC card is useful but shouldn't be relied upon as an alternative to travel insurance. Make sure your insurance policy covers any activities you wish to participate in while on holiday. If you get ill in most of the bigger resorts/towns there is a dedicated medical service *(Guardia Medica Turistica)* for tourists.

EMERGENCY SERVICES
Call 112 – *for the police, fire brigade and ambulance.* Call 80 31 16 (landline); 80 0 11 68 00 (mobile)

INSIDER TIP
Don't be tempted to test the tank!

FESTIVAL & EVENTS
ALL YEAR AROUND

FEBRUARY/MARCH
Carnevale (Barbagia): masquerades and parades.
Sartiglia (Oristano): colourful medieval-style equestrian festival at carnival time.

MARCH/APRIL
Settimana Santa (Cagliari, Alghero, Iglesias): Passion plays around Easter.

APRIL
Skepto (Cagliari): international short film festival, *skepto.net*
Olbia in Fiore The pedestrianised area is turned into a park.

MAY
Sant'Efisio (Cagliari): huge parade in traditional dress (photo).
San Simplicio (Olbia): parades, processions and a riding competition.
Cavalcata Sarda (Sassari): traditional dress and lots of horseriding.
Sardinia Trail (Ogliastra): spectacular trail-running race, *sardiniatrail.com*

EARLY JUNE
Superyacht Regatta (Porto Cervo): international regatta, *yccs.it*

JULY
Sardegna Pride (Cagliari): The city celebrates its LGBTQ residents and visitors!

AUGUST
Musica sulle Bocche (Santa Teresa Gallura): Jazz festival on the beach, *musicasullebocche.it*

SEPTEMBER
San Salvatore (Cabras): barefoot pilgrimage at dawn
Sunandbass (San Teodoro): drum and bass Festival, *sunandbass.net*
Antico Sposalizio Selargino (Selargius): real weddings, traditional dress.

SEPTEMBER–DECEMBER
Autumn in Barbagia (Barbagia): autumn weekend festivals, *cuoredellasardegna.it*

ESSENTIALS

BEACHES

All Sardinian beaches are accessible to the public. Even if there are ever more businesses offering "lido services" (bar, loungers, etc), a part of every beach has to be left to people who aren't interested in such amenities (spiaggia libera). Topless sunbathing is generally tolerated, nudity is generally not.

CREDIT CARDS

There are plenty of ATM cash points (Bancomat); standard credit cards are accepted by most hotels, restaurants, petrol stations and shops. It is not at all unusual for card machines/the network to go down on Sardinia. If so, the card machine will read "POS fuori uso".

ENTRY FEES & PRICES

Admission to state facilities such as museums, archaeological sites, etc. is often much cheaper than in other parts of Europe, and mostly free to those of 18 and under. In fact, it's generally free everywhere on the first Sunday of the month. The range of prices in municipally or privately owned museums is huge. For instance, the Grotta Is Zuddas costs 10 euros, while the Grotta di Nettuno is 13 euros. The famous nuraghic site, Su Nuraxi costs 12 euros, whereas the nuraghic fort of Palmavera and the nuraghe at Losa only cost 5 euros each. The excavated ancient town of Nora costs 7.50 euros while Tharros is 5 euros.

HOW MUCH DOES IT COST?

Coffee	1–1.50 euros for an espresso standing at the counter/bar
Snack	2.50–4 euros for a cheese panino
Wine	2–4 euros for a carafe of vino di casa
Deckchair	5–20 euros/day (in high season and in some places on the Costa Smeralda, this can be significantly more)
Petrol	1.50–1.75 euros for 1 litre super unleaded 95
Bus	6–10 euros for 100km

INFORMATION

sardegnaturismo.it is Sardinia's official tourist website. However, there are of excellent sites and blogs out there, including sardegna.com/en/visit-sardinia/ and italyheaven.co.uk/sardinia.

NATIONAL HOLIDAYS

1 Jan	Capodanno (New Year)
6 Jan	Epifania (Epiphany)
March/April	Pasquetta (Easter Monday)
25 April	Liberazione (Anniversary of the Liberation from Fascism)
1 May	Festa del Lavoro (Labour Day)
2 June	Festa della Repubblica (Republic Day)
15 Aug	Ferragosto (Asuumption Day)

1 Nov	Ognissanti (All Souls' Day)
8 Dec	Immacolata Concezione (Feast of the Immaculate Conception)
25 Dec	Natale (Christmas)
26 Dec	Santo Stefano (Boxing Day/St Stephen's Day)

OPENING TIMES

On weekdays, shops are usually open between 8.30am–1pm and between 5–8pm, markets are generally mornings only. In the high season, many shops will stay open until 10pm or even midnight. Supermarkets and at least one bakery in each village are often open on Sunday mornings.

TELEPHONE & WIFI

The dialling code for the UK is +44, for the US +1 and for Ireland +353. There are no regional dialling codes in Italy so you always have to enter the full number.

Virtually all hotels and campsites have free WiFi. There are hotspots in the airports and many cafes. However, it is still common for holiday lets not to have internet access (or to charge extra for it).

TIPS

Service is automatically included in Sardinian restaurants (servizio compreso). Additional tipping is not necessary but is always appreciated!

TOILETS

Restaurant and bar toilets often leave something to be desired when it comes to cleanliness. It is never a bad idea to have a bit of loo paper and some wet wipes to hand. Don't flush wipes down the loo though, as it can easily lead to blockages.

WEATHER

High season
Low season

	JAN	FEB	MARCH	APRIL	MAY	JUNE	JULY	AUG	SEPT	OCT	NOV	DEC
Daytime temeratures	14°	15°	17°	20°	23°	28°	31°	31°	28°	24°	19°	15°
Night-time temperatures	7°	7°	8°	10°	14°	18°	20°	20°	19°	15°	12°	8°
☀	5	5	6	8	9	10	11	10	8	7	5	4
🌧	7	7	6	5	5	2	1	1	3	6	7	8
≈	14	13	14	15	17	20	23	24	23	21	18	15

☀ Hours of sunshine per day   🌧 Rainfall days per month   ≈ Sea temperature (°C)

USEFUL WORDS & PHRASES

SMALLTALK

Italian uses an accent to indicate that the last syllable is stressed. For other words, we have placed a dot underneath the stressed vowel to help with pronunciation.

Yes/No/Maybe	Sì/No/Forse
Please/Thank you	Per favore/Grazie
Excuse me, please!	Scusa!/Mi scusi
Pardon!/could you repeat?	Come dice?/Prego?
Good morning!/Good afternoon!/Good evening!/Good night!	Buon giorno!/Buon giorno!/Buona sera!/Buona notte!
Hello! / Goodbye!/Bye	Ciao!/Salve! / Arrivederci!/Ciao!
My name is …	Mi chiamo …
What's your name?	Come si chiama?/Come ti chiami?
I would like to …/Have you got …?	Vorrei …/Avete …?
I (don't) like that	(Non) mi piace.
good/bad	buono/cattivo

SYMBOLS

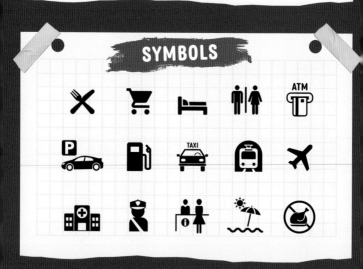

EATING & DRINKING

The menu, please.	Il menù, per favore.
bottle/carafe/glass	bottiglia/caraffa/bicchiere
knife/fork/spoon	coltello/forchetta/cucchiaio
salt/pepper/sugar	sale/pepe/zucchero
vinegar/oil/milk/cream/lemon	aceto/olio/latte/panna/limone
with/without ice/sparkling	con/senza ghiaccio/gas
cold/too salty/not cooked	freddo/troppo salato/non cotto
vegetarian/allergy	vegetariano/vegetariana/allergia
May I have the bill, please?	Vorrei pagare, per favore.
bill/tip	conto/ricevuta/mancia
cash/credit card	in contanti/carta di credito

MISCELLANEOUS

Where can I find...?	Dove posso trovare ...?
left/right/straight ahead/back	sinistra/destra/dritto
What time is it?	Che ora è? Che ore sono?
It is 3 o'clock / half past 3	Sono le tre./Sono le tre e mezza.
today/tomorrow/yesterday	oggi/domani/ieri
How much does... cost?	Quanto costa ...?
too much/a lot/a little/everything/nothing	troppo/molto/poco/tutto/niente
expensive/cheap/price	caro/economico/prezzo
Where can I find somewhere with internet access/WiFi	Dove trovo un accesso internet/wi-fi?
open/closed	aperto/chiuso
broken/not working	guasto/non funziona
breakdown/workshop	guasto/officina
Timetable/ticket	orario/biglietto
train/track/platform	treno/binario/banchina
Help!/Watch out!/Caution!	Aiuto!/Attenzione!/Prudenza!
ban/forbidde/danger/dangerous	divieto/vietato/pericolo/pericoloso
Pharmacy	farmacia
fever/pain	febbre/dolori
0/1/2/3/4/5/6/7/8/9/10/100/1000	zero/uno/due/tre/quattro/cinque /sei/sette/otto/nove/dieci/cento/mille

HOLIDAY VIBES

FOR RELAXATION & CHILLING

FOR BOOKWORMS & FILM BUFFS

📖 SEA AND SARDINIA

D H Lawrence's classic travel book about the island. Written in the aftermath of World War I, Lawrence's enthusiasm for the Sardinian landscape seems as fresh and relevant today as it did then. Worth reading alongside Grazia Deledda's *Reeds in the Wind* to compare the perspectives of a visitor/native.

📖 ACCABADORA

The story of two women in a Sardinian village in the 1950s. Maria is adopted by the ancient Bonnaria, but her new mother is hiding a second life from her – one that is inextricably linked to ancient folk beliefs on the island. A radical novel written in 2009.

🎥 THE SPY WHO LOVED ME

Insane pursuits and races on "wet-bikes" (they were the future once) on the Costa Smeralda. Only James Bond gets to save the world in this kind of luxury! The scenes in Palau's harbour and Capriccioli are particularly memorable!

🎥 ANTHONY BOURDAIN: NO RESERVATIONS

The late Anthony Bourdain's wife is a Sardinian native so his visit to the island is particularly personal. But it is also a celebration of the amazing food on Sardinia and will have you headed to the first trattoria as soon as you arrive on the island!

PLAYLIST

0:58

ǁ ALGHERO – GIUNI RUSSO
Cult '80s classic about a holiday on Sardinia!

▶ NO POTHO REPOSARE
Love song from the 1920s that will bring tears to the eyes of any homesick Sardinian.

▶ NANNEDDU MEU
A poem put to music, which mourns for the old days. Heard at every Sardinian folk festival.

▶ HOTEL SUPRAMONTE – **FABRIZIO DE ANDRÈ**
A surprisingly sentimental look at the songwriter's own experience of being taken hostage in 1979

▶ DUSTY KID – INNU
Electro mixed with *launeddas* and *mamuthones*' sounds.

▶ DOMO MIA
Eros Ramazzotti tries his hand at Sardinian in this collaboration with the island's native Tazenda.

Your holiday soundtrack can be found on **Spotify** under **MARCO POLO Italy**

Or scan this code with the Spotify app

ONLINE

INSTAGRAM.COM/ FABRIZIO_BIBI_PINNA
Fabrizio and his lovely lab Farah get around the island a lot, exploring the best places for those with two legs … and those with four.

COAST APP
A very good guide to the beaches and events in Olbia and along the Costa Smeralda.

DITZIONARIU. SARDEGNACULTURA.IT
A dictionary which also explains expressions particular to Sardinia and its native languages. Can be set to many languages; English is of course among them.

PLUS.GOOGLE.COM/+ALDOBBIT
Aldo has a B & B near Arzachena but is better known online for his drone and GoPro videos. Video blogging at its (rare) best.

TRAVEL PURSUIT

THE MARCO POLO HOLIDAY QUIZ

Do you know what makes Sardinia tick? Test your knowledge of the island's hidden secrets and quirks here. The answers are at the bottom of the page with more information on pages 18–23.

❶ Which of these are there most of on Sardinia?
a) Nuraghi
b) Sheep
c) People

❷ What is Sardinian?
a) A mixture of Catalan and Italian only spoken in Alghero
b) A native language
c) The dialect of Italian spoken on Sardinia

❸ What is not produced from cork on the island?
a) Mousepads
b) Designer fashion
c) Cushions

❹ What do Sardinian murals generally depict?
a) News stories and political satire
b) Sardinian natural scenes and beaches
c) Religious allegories

❺ What is on the Sardinian flag?
a) The outline of the island
b) The silhouettes of four Moors
c) A stylised sun

❻ Which wind on the north and west coasts is particularly popular with surfers and windsurfers?
a) Shirokko
b) Mistral
c) Bora

How many shepherds tend Sardinia's numerous sheep? Check out question 13!

❼ What is the most expensive area of Sardinia called?
a) Costa Concordia
b) Costa Smeralda
c) Costa Rei

❽ Which village was once the most infamous home of bandits on the island?
a) Corleone
b) Siligo
c) Orgosolo

❾ What do tourists who arrive in Porto Torres on the ferry see first when they reach the island?
a) The biggest nuraghic fort on the island
b) A NATO base and exercise yard
c) Oil refineries

❿ What are there more than 7,000 of on Sardinia?
a) Nuraghi
b) Beach bars
c) Cork producers

⓫ The approx. 100 Saracen towers were built to protect the island from what?
a) The spread of large fires
b) Pirate attacks
c) Attacks from enemy villages

⓬ Which of the following is a popular export from Sardinia?
a) Sea salt
b) Sheep's cheese
c) Sand

⓭ How many shepherds are there on Sardinia?
a) about 9,000
b) about 30,000
c) about 55,000

INDEX

Credits

Cover Picture: Capo d'Orso (Schapowalow/SIME: M. Arduino)
Photos: DuMont image archive: C. & T. Anzenberger (Front flap, inside and outside, 1, 11, 19, 24/25, 26/27, 30/31, 35, 49, 54/55, 60, 62, 64, 67, 73, 74/75, 78, 82, 89, 103, 109, 110/111, 120, 134/135, 137, 144/145); R. M. Gill (31); P. Höh (127); Huber images: M. Arduino (124/125); huber-images: A. Addis (27), D. Erbetta (51), O. Fantuz (98/99), J. Huber (42); huber-images/Spexi: A. Addis (56/57, 61, 93); Laif: H.-B. Huber (130), D. Schmid (9); Laif/hemis.fr: L. Montico (38/39); Look/age fotostock (119); T. Lutz (147); mauritius images: C. Bäck (85); mauritius images/age fotostock: J. Wlodarczyk (107); mauritius images/age fotostock/ Clickalps SRLs (4/5, 14/15); mauritius images/Alamy: N. Iacono (8), M. Spanu (12/13); mauritius images/ClickAlps (2/3); mauritius images/CuboImages: R. Lombardo (123), L. Picciau (117); mauritius images/CuboImages (132, E. Spanu (115); mauritius images/CuboImges: L. Picciau (87); mauritius images/Cultura: D. Fettes (95), S. Oppo (10); mauritius images/Travel Collection (53); mauritius images/United Archives: DeAgostini (46); Schapowalow Images: A. Addis (32/33, 45, 68/69), U. Bernhart (23), O. Fantuz (142/143), T. & B. Morandi (20), R. Spila (104); Schapowalow: V. Leplat (121); O. Stadler (96); vario images/imagebroker (81); T. Widmann (71)

3rd Edition – fully revised and updated 2022
Worldwide Distribution: Heartwood Publishing Ltd, Bath, United Kingdom
www.heartwoodpublishing.co.uk

© MAIRDUMONT GmbH & Co. KG, Ostfildern
Authors: Hans Bausenhardt, Timo Lutz
Editor: Nikolai Michaelis
Picture editor: Gabriele Forst
Cartography: © MAIRDUMONT, Ostfildern (pp. 36–37, 126, 129, 133, outer flap, pull-out map) © MAIRDUMONT, Ostfildern, using data from OpenStreetMap, Licence CC-BY-SA 2.0 (pp. 40–41, 58–59, 63, 66, 76–77, 90, 100–101, 112–113, 114).
Cover, wallet and pull-out map design: bilekjaeger_Kreativagentur with Zukunftswerkstatt, Stuttgart
Page design: Langenstein Communication GmbH, Ludwigsburg

Heartwood Publishing credits:
Translated from the German by Sophie Blacksell Jones, John Owen and Susan Jones
Editors: Felicity Laughton and Kate Michell
Prepress: Summerlane Books, Bath
Printed in India

MARCO POLO AUTHOR
TIMO LUTZ

Born in southwest Germany, Timo studied in Saxony before getting stranded on Sardinia. He has now been there for more than two decades and has never lost his passion for the island. As a travel journalist, he spends a lot of time making sure he knows which bays are the best and which mountains have the finest views. His only problem in his chosen home? Coming from a landlocked corner of Germany, he is still not a big fan of fish!